Miracles Among The Cowboys!

By Ronnie Christian

Presenting Jesus
- He Still Cares -

Pen In My Hand Publishing

Miracles Among The Cowboys!

Text Copyright © 2009 Ronnie Christian
www.christiancowboy.org
First Printing 2009

Pen In My Hand Publishing
P.O. Box 187, Blanco, Texas 78606
www.christiancowboy.org
For more information contact:
Christian Cowboys and Friends
P.O. Box 187, Blanco, Texas 78606
(830) 386-4936

Manufactured in the United States of America

ISBN: 978-0-9770325-1-8
Library of Congress Control Number:

- "New Testament Scriptures taken from the New American Standard Bible®, Copyright 1960, 1962, 1963, 1968, 1971, 1972, 1973, 1975, 1977, 1995, by The Lockman Foundation. Used by permission." (www.Lockman.org).
- Old Testament Scriptures are from the New King James Version unless otherwise noted. Those from the King James Version will have (KJ) after the verses.

Contributing Writers and witnesses - See Chapters 9, 18, 24, 25 and part of 17
Layout and Design by: Tammy Zamorano, Kerrville, Texas

INTRODUCTION: My name is Ronnie Christian. I am a rodeo cowboy who loves Jesus and wants to bring others to know Him. I am a member of the Professional Rodeo Cowboys Association.

VISION: Reach rodeo cowboys and cowgirls with the Good News that Jesus loves them and Jesus Saves. Through this, their families, friends, and the many people they contact around the world, including ranchers and others in the horse and livestock industry will know God cares for them and Jesus is Lord.

EXPECTATION: See people saved, set free, healed spiritually, physically, and emotionally, filled with the Holy Spirit, and living a life pleasing to God.

My thanks go to Glenn and Ann Smith of International Western World Outreach Center, aka Rodeo Cowboy Ministries and Coy and Donna Huffman of Cowboy Church International, aka Pro Rodeo Ministries for speaking into my life and encouraging me to believe that the word of God is active in the affairs of people today. They showed me that the name of Jesus still produces signs, wonders, blessings and miracles when we do what Jesus tells us to do in the Bible.

Miracles Among The Cowboys!

Foreword

Jesus Is A Miracle Worker!

Hebrews 13:8 "Jesus Christ is the same yesterday and today, yes and forever."

That means He is still doing what He has always done. He is still healing broken bodies, broken hearts, and broken dreams. Jesus is the Healer. He is still active in the affairs of people on earth.

We see people healed, horses healed, people receiving peace in their hearts and confusion leaving their minds. We speak blessings in Jesus Name. Although we do pray over people at times - most of the time we speak the answer. That is what Jesus did. I'm not sure if He ever prayed over anyone. He would go pray to the Father - then He would come out speaking blessings - "Be healed." Be still! "Your faith has saved you." "Go in peace." "Be gone (to the devil and demons)." "Peace be with you." He gave us instructions in *Mark 11:22-23* *"...Have faith in God (23) Truly, I say to you "Whoever says to this mountain, 'Be taken up and cast into the sea, and does not doubt in his heart, but believes that what he says is going to happen, he shall have what he says.'"* (combination of NAS/NKJ). Verse 24 goes on to tell us that when we pray and ask, believe and we will receive. We are also told in *Mat. 7:7 "Ask and it shall be given."* Also in *John 16:23-24 We are to ask the Father in Jesus Name for our requests to come into being..."*

So we can and certainly do pray but much of the time we should be speaking the blessing by faith.

That is what Jesus did and we are told to do the works that He did in *John 14:12* *"Truly, truly, I say to you, he who believes in Me, the works that I do, he shall do also; and greater works than these he shall do; because I go to the Father."* Jesus always spoke life. Everywhere Jesus went He spoke blessings. He said in *John 6:63* *"It is the Spirit who gives life; the flesh profits nothing; the words that I have spoken to you are spirit and life."* Speak life everywhere you go!

What happened when Jesus spoke? The blind saw, the crippled walked, the sick were healed, demons were cast out; the dead were raised to life. Even the wind obeyed Him. And the good news of the kingdom of God was preached.

When Jesus spoke, things changed. When we speak in His name things should and do change.

In this book are some miracle stories of Jesus power working in cowboys' and cowgirls' lives today just as we read about in the Bible.

Very important note! God is no respecter of persons. He is not partial. What He does for cowboys and cowgirls and others He will do for you. Don't limit God! Speak life! Speak blessings! Speak the miraculous! See miracles! You will see miracles in your life and in the lives of those around you.

NOTE: The reports of the miracles in this book were witnessed by the author and other contributors to this book who are known by the author. Also they were confirmed by the people involved in the reports. I hope they encourage you to believe and receive miracles in your life.

Table Of Contents

(Chapters 9, 18, 24, 25 and part of 17 were contributed by others than the Author).

chapter

1

Pickup Man's Horse Bowed Tendon Healed

Lance Crump, the pickup man at the Bay City Texas PRCA Rodeo said to me, "Ronnie, my horse just pulled up crippled. Go pray over him." (A pickup man moves in to get the riders off of the bucking horses and he moves animals out of the arena). He was still in the arena doing his job on different horses. I left the arena to go out back to the horse stalls. When I found the horse I got down on one knee and put my hands on his leg. He put his mouth down to smell my hands. A well known team roper, Tom Wren, rode by and I said, "Look!" He took one quick glance and said, "Bowed tendon." This takes horses out of action. I kept my hands on his leg. The horse put his nose on my hands to smell me again. Then I said, "I speak to your bones, ligaments and tendons to line up with the word of God, I call every cell and fiber in your body to be healed in Jesus name. The next morning I saw Candi, the pickup man's wife. They are both believers in Jesus and in His miracle working power. I said, "Let's go pray over that horse again." ("Speak healing to that horse's leg again" would have been more accurate.) We went to his stall and again I went and laid hands and spoke life and healing. His wife prayed in agreement with me. *Mat. 18:19 "Again I say to you, that if two of you agree on earth about anything that they may ask, it shall be done for them by My Father who is in heaven."*

The next week at another rodeo I saw Lance and he told me, "Ronnie that horse is healed. I can ride him and use him." I asked, "Where is he? I want to see him." He replied, "I left him at home this week. I am riding some other horses here, but he is totally healed and ready to go."

1

chapter
2

M.S. Goes
At The Rodeo School

In the spring of 2002 a rodeo producer and stock contractor, Lester Meier, sponsored a free two day Bareback Riding School.

The first night I announced that we would have a Cowboy Church service in the morning. Then I went ahead and preached about a ten minute message that night. Ten students (teenagers) prayed to receive Jesus as Savior. So we had the greatest miracle which is to have your sins forgiven, become a member of God's family and to have eternal life received with heaven as your home.

The next morning we gathered in the rodeo grandstands. There was about 40-50 people including the students, instructor, the workers and their families. I preached on "Don't Limit God". I mentioned Psalm 78:41. "Yes, again and again they tempted God, and limited the Holy One of Israel." Again ten more received Jesus as Savior. Praise God!

As the group began making their way back to the arena for more rodeo instruction, more practice and to ride more bucking horses, one lady held back. Her son was a student in the school. She came over to me and said, "It's time to start doing what you were talking about." I said, "What's that?" She said, "It's time for me to stop limiting God." I asked, "What's wrong?" She replied, "I have M.S. (multiple sclerosis)." I didn't know exactly what MS is or what it does but I knew the disease had something to do with the muscles. I laid a hand on her shoulder and quietly said something like, "I command these muscles to line up with the word of God, every cell and fiber and tissue. Be healed in Jesus name. Amen."

I put the sound system away and went back to the arena to help with the bareback riding.

When the school was over a few hours later I walked over to the lady and said, "How are you doing?" She joyfully replied, "I am doing things that I couldn't do before!" Her husband smiled and interjected, "I used to have to help her up and down the grandstands. She has been running up and down them on her on all afternoon."

A few months later I saw her son at another rodeo school. I asked, "How is your mother doing?" He replied, "She is having some trouble with her heart." I told him, "You tell your mother, the same God who healed her of M.S. will heal her heart too." I saw her and the family on several occasions over the next few years. She is healthy and they never mentioned her heart condition again.

I saw her about a year after the first school and asked her if what I had reported about this incident was true. She read our ministries' newsletters telling about her healing. She said, "Ronnie, when you prayed (although I didn't pray I just spoke) I was healed instantly but it took about a year for me to get my strength back. I have gone back to work."

The next year I saw her later at the annual rodeo in her hometown. As we were talking I dropped my Bible bag. She very quickly bent over and picked it up off the ground and handed it back to me. Then she excitedly said with a smile, "You know I couldn't do that before!"

I see her now about once or twice a year. She is doing great - totally healed - and is stronger every year I see her. She and her husband always come with a big smile and visit me when they see me at a rodeo. They are still very thankful to God for her healing. She has her health and her job and her joy. *III John 2 "Beloved, I pray that in all respects you may prosper and be in good health, just as your soul prospers."*

Bull Riders' Knees Healed

Mark 16:15-20 And He said to them, "Go into all the world and preach the gospel to all creation. (16) He who has believed and has been baptized shall be saved; but he who has disbelieved shall be condemned. (17) These signs will accompany those who have believed: in My name they will cast out demons, they will speak with new tongues; (18) they will pick up serpents, and if they drink any deadly poison, it will not hurt them; they will lay hands on the sick and they will recover." (19) So then, when the Lord Jesus had spoken to them, He was received up into heaven and sat down at the right hand of God. (20) And they went out and preached everywhere, while the Lord worked with them, and confirmed the word by the signs that followed.

It says above that these "signs will accompany <u>those who believe</u>", not just preachers or someone with the gift of healing or the gift of miracles.

When I was the pastor at Cowboy Church - Bandera in Bandera, Texas, I had the people come up one night to encourage them to believe that God would use them for healing. I laid my hands on each of their hands and encouraged them to use their hands - to lay their hands on the sick and expect them to recover.

About a week later I was at the Professional Bull Riders (PBR) Finals in Las Vegas, Nevada at Thomas and Mack Sports Arena. A World Champion Bull Rider, Terry Don West, made a great ride. He was marked in the 90's and won some money, but when he was on the ground after the ride he had trouble getting to his feet to walk out of the arena. I was sitting next to a well known orthopedic surgeon that has taken care of and operated on many of the bull riders. I said, "What 's wrong? Is it his back?" He replied, "No, it's his knee."

I went back to the dressing room area. Terry Don was in the narrow hallway outside of the dressing room. I went over to him and said, "Terry Don, the Bible says these signs shall follow them that believe, they shall lay hands on the sick and they shall recover. I just prayed over the hands of the people in my church last week to be used for healing and I received that same prayer for myself. I put my hand on his shoulder. People were walking past us on both sides. I said, "Don't bow your head, don't close your eyes, just listen." Then I spoke to his body to line up with the Word of God. I said (something like), I command this body to line up with the Word of God, every muscle, ligament, tendon; every cell, tissue and every fiber and nerve ending, "line up with the Word of God - In Jesus Name." We parted.

I watched from a distance over the next three performances as Terry Don made some super rides. His score was 90 plus once or twice again. (A 90 plus is very high in the bull riding). He had a good Finals, won some money and left healthy.

The next day I was eating breakfast with some friends. Terry Don, the now healed bull rider, walked over to the table. He spoke quietly to me and said, "You know Ronnie, when you prayed over me I thought, 'It's just going to have to hurt.'" Then he grinned and said, "Didn't feel a thing." He was totally healed and pain free. He was able to perform in the arena, make good bull rides, win some money, have a profitable Finals and leave there praising God for his healing and success.

A couple of weeks went by and I went to a smaller bull riding in Kerrville, Texas - the Annual Johnny Nix Memorial Bull Riding.

I saw another bull rider, Ronny Kitchens, who won the very first PBR Finals average in Las Vegas a few years earlier. He had a terribly bad messed up knee. He had torn ligaments and tendons the previous year. It was a nasty injury. But here he was back ready to ride again. I asked him, "How is your knee?" He answered, "It's not 100% but I'm starting to ride with it." I told him about what had happened at the PBR Finals two weeks prior with Terry Don. Then I said, "Ronny, God is no respecter of persons." He looked at me with a curious look. I said, "Do you know what that means?" He answered, "No." I replied, "He's not partial." Then Ronny lit up and said, "You mean God loves me just as much as Terry Don?" I answered, "Yeah." He said, "Get over here and pray over me too!" I laid hands on him and spoke the same type of words over Ronny as I did over Terry Don.

Ronny rode his bull shortly after that - well actually he got on but bucked off before the eight second horn. After the bull riding was over I was talking with a guy about his relationship with Jesus. It turns out that Ronny rode to the bull riding in this person's car. I presented Jesus to the man as I had in the past. This time was different though. He bowed his head and I lead him in a prayer to receive Jesus into his heart to be his Savior and Lord. Praise God! The greatest miracle just happened. His sins were forgiven, he now had heaven and eternal life to look forward to.

Ronny walked up about that time with his gear bag. He was ready to leave. I told him about his friend's decision. They were walking off toward the exit and I thought I would ask Ronny if he was healed. Then I thought, "No, if he is healed, he will tell me." Then I looked and Ronny was coming back toward me. When he got to me he said (something like), "If I land on my head, my butt or my elbow, my knee hurts. Tonight I landed on my knee. It didn't hurt." Although he did not win anything in the bull riding that night, he left healed, touched by our mighty God and ready to ride in the future in good physical condition.

Ronny went on to ride and do well again as a bull rider for several years since that night.

Once more - a <u>miracle among the cowboys</u>! We rejoice to still see Jesus the Healer in our midst taking care of His people.

chapter 4

Torn Groin Muscle - No Pain!

In about 1981 I (the author, Ronnie Christian) was stretching just before I rode my bareback horse at the Jacksonville, TX. PRCA Rodeo. I felt something pop and a sick feeling hit me in the pit of my stomach. Most cowboys have strained and pulled their groin muscle at sometime in their career - I knew this was different. It was torn! I quickly wrapped my groin with a stretch material type bandage and got on the horse. About five or six seconds into the ride the pain was too much; I was not riding well so I jumped off the horse. (A rider must ride eight seconds to qualify for a score).

I had just come off a previous week of first place wins in Santa Fe, New Mexico and a small town in Kansas. I was riding well. My confidence was up. I was healthy. Life was good.

The next night I tried to ride with my groin wrapped again. I had a good horse and was making a good ride. It looked like I would leave that rodeo sitting in first place but right at eight seconds as the whistle blew, the pain was tremendous so I reached down with my free hand. (Note: to touch the animal with your free hand or try to ride with both hands is a rule infraction - to do this results in a zero - no score - no win - no money). It was a close call. One judge marked my ride (gave me a score), the others judge felt that I reached down and grabbed the horse's mane before the whistle.

My car was packed for a long trip for myself and the family. We were going to the big rodeo - "The Daddy of 'em all" in Cheyenne, Wy. plus other rodeos in Salt Lake City and Ogden, Utah that week. Plans can change very quickly. I knew I had to go home and heal to be able to ride and win.

As I was leaving the rodeo arena I looked at a well known bull rider and said, "Bobby, God gave me two things - faith and wis-

8

dom. My wisdom says go home and heal up. I turned to leave but froze in my tracks and turned back around and I said to him, "But my faith says it won't be long!"

Before I left the rodeo a bull rider told me, "Ronnie it will take at least three months to heal." Another bull rider and calf roper friend of mine said, "I tore my groin. It took a year to heal." So we were a bit down and decided to go home.

On the way home I said, "We are not going to let the devil steal our joy we experienced last week. *All things work together for good for those who love God and are called according to His purpose.*" (That is Romans 8:28 which came to my mind).

That week at home I sold a piece of property that I really needed to sell and used the proceeds to pay some bills. The negotiations were with a man with a very unusual and hard to deal with personality. But the sale was completed and I received funding. Praise God!

However, I still was entered in the Cheyenne PRCA Rodeo the following weekend and I had not called in to turn out (cancel my ride) with a medical release. I went to a church in Huntsville, Texas, a different one than where I usually attended. I thought, "I am going somewhere where they believe God still heals and answers prayer." That night at the end of the service the pastor said, "If anyone needs healing come up to be prayed for." I started to go forward and it was like my feet were stuck to the ground. I felt like the Lord spoke to me and said, "I know when you are up at Cheyenne, you can still work your real estate job like you are." So I did not go up for prayer at that time.

But I did something else. I began to eat (devour, read) healing Scriptures all week. A few month's earlier I had watched the movie, "Chariots of Fire." When the track star, Eric Liddell, would not run in the Sunday race in the Olympics; he instead spoke at a church. One Scripture passage he used was in *Isaiah 40:29-31*

9

(29) He gives power to the weak, and to those who have no might He increases strength. (30) Even the youths shall faint and be weary, and the young men shall utterly fall. (31) But those who wait on the Lord shall renew their strength; they shall mount up with wings like eagles, they shall run and not be weary, they shall walk and not faint." During the movie I had taken out a small piece of paper and scribbled Isaiah 40 and tucked it away in my wallet. That was one Scripture I meditated on during the week. I "ate" other Scriptures like *I Peter 2:24 "...by His stripes you were healed." plus Mt. 8:17 "...He Himself took our infirmities and carried away our diseases."*

The more of the Word I read concerning my healing the more my faith grew. I packed the car I was driving again and began the over 1,000 plus mile trip from Texas to ride in Cheyenne, Wyoming on Saturday, only eight days after I had torn my groin. As we drove I "ate" healing Scriptures all the way there as I had for the previous week.

Besides riding at the Cheyenne Rodeo, I also was to be inducted as President of the Cowboy Chapter of the Fellowship of Christian Athletes (now known as the Fellowship of Christian Cowboys). Of course my mind would say, "You don't have to be healed to take the position of President. You can go to Cheyenne just for that only." But my spirit man inside and the greater One who lives in me believed for more.

Finally it was time to ride. At the motel about three hours before the rodeo I picked up a Bible and read *Hebrews 13:8 "Jesus Christ is the same yesterday and today, yes, and forever."* I said, "That settles it. Let's go to the rodeo and ride." I did ride that day and I was winning the first Go-round when the day was done. (I finished the go-round in second place).

I was shouting, "Praise the Lord!" The cowboys around me thought it was because I was winning the rodeo but I was saying,

10

"Praise the Lord!" because my groin did not hurt - no pain!

I went that night to another rodeo in Colorado a few hours south of Cheyenne, WY. I had a good bucking horse, made a good spur ride - again - no pain! I won money at both rodeos.

The Justin Sports Medicine trainer looked at my groin a few weeks later at the Colorado Springs, Colorado PRCA Pikes Peak or Bust Rodeo. There was a dip in my muscle up high where the groin attaches. He said, "Well, Ronnie, it started to tear, it just stopped." Then he showed me a better way to stretch before my rides. Their is still a dip in the groin muscle area. I went on to ride hundreds of times over the next ten years with no pain in my groin ever. God did not reattach the muscle to the original condition - but He did strengthen me, took the pain away and kept if from tearing further. I wrapped my groin with a sports groin wrap for about a year but I never had any pains. I finally threw the wrap away.

The dip in my groin now reminds me of how God strengthened my body, took the pain away and allowed me to be pain free all these years from the injury. There is a lot of strain on your groin when you ride bareback bucking horses and bulls. Miracle - you decide. I know this, I was in pain, I trusted God as my healer, I rode in eight days at a level where I could win. I had no pain or problem ever again with my groin. Now I tell people when they are sick or injured if they do not receive a quick miraculous healing, "Eat healing Scriptures; when you believe the Word more than your pain, the pain will leave." God did it for me - He will do it for you!

chapter

5

Instantly Set Free!

At the big Cheyenne, Wyoming PRCA Rodeo held every July we had Bible Studies, prayer meetings and Cowboy Church nightly in the horse barns for years in the late 1970's and into the 80's.

One night two couples came to the meeting. We did not know them very well. One of the cowboys, Mike Fletcher, who was a champion saddle bronc rider in another association, had decided to step up to competing in the PRCA.

That night he and his wife, Darlene, prayed and made a fresh commitment to serve Jesus as Savior and Lord. They now wanted their lifestyle to show that they were believers in Jesus and to be pleasing to Him. It was time to let Jesus to be in control. They walked out of darkness to light, out of sin to right standing with God. They had already received Jesus and had come out of death to life out of hell to heaven, out of eternal death to eternal life. **What a blessing - this is truly the greatest miracle we can experience!** God becomes your Father - your body becomes a temple of the Holy Spirit. *John 3:16 "For God so loved the world that He gave His only begotten Son, that whoever believes in Him should not perish but have everlasting life." (NKJ) and John 3:36 "He who believes in the Son has everlasting life; and he who does not believe the Son shall not see life, but the wrath of God abides in him." (NKJ)* Also see *Romans 10:13 "for 'whoever calls on the name of the Lord shall be saved.'"*

They were now ready to start serving Jesus more seriously. They desired to be baptized in the Holy Spirit. They desired more power to be used by God.

Cowboy preacher, Coy Huffman, and some others of us prayed with the four again after most of the other people left. I felt like others were around that little group - it seemed like we had company - I felt like angels were around us although I saw no one

12

else.

All four, the Fletcher's and the other couple, were baptized with the Holy Spirit and spoke in tongues like the new believers did in Acts 10:42-46. Darlene went off to sit on the bleacher; A lady sat down next to her. Darlene would pray out loud in tongues, then say, "I don't need it anymore." Then she would pray in tongues and say again, "I don't need it anymore." Finally the lady asked her, "Honey, what is it you don't need anymore?" She responded, "The drugs! I don't need it anymore!" She was instantly set free from drug use.

At the next rodeo in Dodge City, Kansas her friends came to her and asked, "What are you on?" (Of course they meant what drug?) She answered, "Jesus!" They went away puzzled.

Mike and Darlene began to grow in Christ; they stayed excited about Jesus. They got under a good pastor when they moved to Florida. They got involved in Bible Study and church. In time they began a ministry. They brought city kids to their property to ride horses and teach them about Jesus.

Mike's career lasted over 20 more years as a saddle bronc rider. Darlene rode and trained barrel horses. He went on to win his Circuit Championship and qualify and ride in the PRCA Dodge National Circuit Finals Rodeo for many years. This couple has been a light for Jesus and helped many others over the years in their walk with God.

They are still active in the rodeo business - he is a pick-up man at rodeos and she is a timer and rodeo secretary.

They still serve Jesus 25 years later and are a blessing to the world.

What a miracle - salvation, Spirit filled, set free from drug use, in ministry, serving God and bringing others to know Jesus.

Two miraculously changed lives! Praise God! *Romans 6:11 "Even so consider yourselves dead to sin, but alive to God in Christ Jesus."*

chapter

6

Colic In Horse Healed/ Salvation Comes

I had been invited to hold a Cowboy Church service at a youth rodeo in Cotulla, Texas (in south Texas). A well-known barrel racer, who was the rodeo secretary and a rodeo committee official, invited me to come. Her husband was a steer roper. Her daughter was entered in the youth rodeo barrel racing event. Her brother was a calf roper. Her parents were ranchers in the horse and cattle business, plus they brought in hunters for wild game hunting. The whole family had grown up taking care of animals.

I drove several miles down a very bumpy road to the ranch. It was dark and I had never been there before; I arrived at about 10 p.m. on Saturday night. I had driven several hours that day and night, and was feeling a little tired. When I got out of the car, my host who invited me came over to me leading her barrel racing horse. She said, "Ronnie lay your hands on this horse, he has colic." (Colic is a twisted intestine. Horses die from this.) Well her faith was up, so I did as she said. We laid hands on her horse and prayed that God would heal it.   Glenn Smith, a cowboy preacher, told me one time, "Ronnie the Bible says lay hands on the sick and they will recover - it doesn't say sick people, it just says the sick." God does not like sick - not sick people, not sick animals.

After praying over the horse the girl's dad said, "Do you want me to put him in the stall and keep an eye on him?" She responded to my surprise, "No, Ronnie prayed over him, he's okay. Let's go into the house and have the birthday party. (It was her young son's birthday. I don't remember exactly, but I think he was about 3 to 4 years of age). So they turned the horse out into an exercise arena near the horse barn. We went inside, ate supper, had a birthday party, and went to bed.

The next day her father, the rancher was at Cowboy Church. He was about 70 plus years old I believe. His sister, also in her 70's, attended.

I preached the message "Stay Excited About Jesus"; I told how Jesus is still active in the affairs of men and women, boys and girls in today's world. I am sure I must have quoted *Hebrews 13:8 "Jesus Christ is the same yesterday and today, yes and forever."* I told them not to limit God. I told them I am excited about Jesus because He still heals the sick, heals broken hearts and broken dreams, changes people for the good, He still saves and brings us to the Father in Heaven. He alone provides us with eternal life.

That rancher, that day, prayed to accept Jesus as his Savior and Lord. His sister did too. He told me, "I don't sleep real good at night; I get up and read books, then I go back to bed. But if there is a sick animal on my place, I get up every hour on the hour to check on them. Last night I slept through the whole night without waking up. This morning I checked on that horse and he was totally healed." That made such an impression on this rancher that God would heal his horse that he was very attentive at church that morning. He listened about **how to really know God - not just about Him** and not just about stories that happened two thousand years ago. He received Jesus and eternal life right there in those rodeo grand stands. He was smiling, and had the joy and peace of God on him. His sister received Jesus also.

Next he says to me, "The next time I have a sick animal I am going to call you to come pray for them." I said, "You don't have to. You're a believer. The Bible says, 'these signs will follow them that believe: they will lay hands on the sick and they will recover.' It doesn't say preachers, it says believers. You are a believer, you lay "your" hands on the sick and pray."

His daughter, my host, was at the rodeo secretary office taking entries during this time so I went by to let her know that her Dad received Jesus that morning. Everyone rejoiced! It was indeed a good weekend. Her best horse was healed and she was able to use him at many more rodeos. Her dad is now saved and has a home in heaven. Often in the Bible, Jesus would heal people, the crowds would come, and then He would tell them about the kingdom of God. He healed them because of His compassion, but He also used it as an opportunity to save souls. That's what we saw here. We went from healing to salvation of a man and his sister!

chapter

7

Bareback Rider -
Took The Neck Brace Off
Mark Gomes,
A World Champion Bareback Rider

I befriended World Champion Bareback Rider, Mark Gomes, at the Turquoise Circuit Finals Rodeo in Bullhead City, Arizona in 1995. He was young as a Christian but ready to learn and grow in Christ.

The next month I saw him at the San Antonio, Texas PRCA Rodeo. He had a neck brace on when he rode which is not uncommon for cowboys in that event. We decided to meet after the rodeo at a nearby truck stop to eat supper and visit after the rodeo.

We met several hours after the bareback riding and he was still wearing his neck brace. Most bareback riders don't wear their neck brace to a restaurant. After eating, we were visiting in the parking lot with his traveling partner, Jeff Collins, another Christian bareback rider. I asked, "Why do you still have your neck brace on?" He told me that his neck was so sore he had to wear it much of the time.

I looked at him, and his partner and said something like, Jesus is the healer. I thought about anointing him with oil and praying over him. But instead this Scripture came to my remembrance and I told them, *Matthew 18:19 "...if two of you agree on earth about anything that they may ask, it shall be done for them by My Father who is in heaven."* and also *Mark 16:17 "And these signs will accompany those who have believed... (18) ...they will lay hands on the sick and they will recover."* You could see it in their faces that they were taking hold of what I said.

Then I looked at Jeff and asked, "You are a believer, aren't

17

you?" He said, "Yes." I said, "Well let's lay hands on him and pray." We did and soon he was not wearing the brace (except when he rode bucking horses).

Later that year or the next we called to interview Mark. He said, "I wished some non-believers would have been there. God healed my neck."

Also since becoming a Christian his attitude about life improved. He was now "Happy in the Lord" which was the title of the interview.

A few years later Mark received what could have been a career ending injury and could have hindered him all of his life. A bucking horse flipped in the chute and broke his pelvis, among other injuries. He knew Jesus is the healer, but this injury was going to be a slower healing. However God is good; the next year Mark was riding in championship form again and qualified for the Wrangler National Finals Rodeo as a contender for a another world title. He slowed a bit in his travels after that but continued to ride and win for several years more. He is still active in rodeo and also ropes and trains horses.

Ps. 31:14 But as for me, I trust You, O Lord; I say, "You are my God" (15) My times are in Your hands..."

We are in good hands - and this is one bareback rider who says, "Thank You Lord."

(Note: As a matter of fact, I talked with him a few years after his bad accident, and we were talking about praying. He said, "Oh, Ronnie I don't ever ask God for anything anymore, I just thank Him for what He gives me." After the rodeo that night, he and several other contestants met with me back in the dressing room just to give God thanks for being with everyone at the rodeo that night and for His protection.)

chapter

8

Goliath And The Bone Chips

The bareback instructor, Jim Richards, at a free Bareback Riding School (hosted by rodeo stock contractor Lester Meier) was using his daughter's horse as a pick up horse. He is a very large grey horse, about seventeen hands tall with large bones. He just seemed to stand out among the other horses. They named him Goliath.

The instructor, and his wife, Kay, got the horse for their sixteen year old daughter, Deana Michelle. He was to be her barrel racing horse.

Goliath came from Tennessee to Texas on a truck with sixteen other horses. He was bruised a bit and sore when he arrived. So they put him out to pasture for a few months.

Then they took him to a veterinarian. X-rays showed that he had a bone chip in his leg pulling off from the rest of the bone. It was in his right front knee. The vet said, "He will never run again." They put him out to pasture again for about six to eight months, then tried to run him again." The swelling came back.

A second veterinarian checked him and took several x-rays. He said it would take surgery to take care of the problem at a cost of $3,500.

They waited three months and took the horse to the rodeo school. They thought maybe he could handle being a pickup man's horse and not re-injure the leg. They felt like the strain of running and turning in the barrel racing was still too much on the horse's injured leg.

We held a Cowboy Church service for all of the students, workers and their families on Sunday, the second day of the school. The daughter attended. She prayed to receive Jesus as her

Lord and Savior that day. I think she had done that before perhaps, but this day she made a commitment to put Him first in her life, to be more serious about the things of God, to go to another level and serve Jesus with her whole heart.

After the service she brought the horse to me. I spoke healing to his leg, his bones, his ligaments and muscles. They had prayed before but she felt it was different this time.

When she got home she told her mother, "We've prayed before for Goliath but I think something is happening this time." The thickness in his leg began to go down. The vet had said he would never run again, but when three months went by the Richards' decided to take Goliath back to the vet. He asked, "Which leg is it?" He did not remember. They told him the right leg. He responded, "It can't be. It must be the other leg. I can't believe it." They said, "It was the right leg that was hurt." New x-rays showed that Goliath has no bone chips. Praise God! Final statement by the Vet, "Go run him! He can barrel race!" Now there is no swelling, no limp and no lameness. His whole spirit has changed. His attitude is better. He has never been the same.

Their daughter's spirit changed too. Her attitude on life and in life improved. Her school grades went up. Her trust in God increased. The whole Richards' family gives glory to God for healing their horse.

God loves us and He loves our animals too. Go Goliath - run with all your might!

(This family had experienced God's healing power before when the dad broke his neck in the bareback riding event at a rodeo. He was healed and rode again for several more years - see story in the next chapter).

chapter
9

Quadriplegic Rides Again

As told by Jim and Kay Richards
Doctor's Report: Broken Neck/Quadriplegic
God's Report: Go Ride Again
Result: Broken Neck Healed -Bareback Rider Rides
And Wins Again. Pain Free!

Jim Richards, a bareback rider at rodeos, had been riding bucking horses since 1970 and was still going strong. But at a rodeo in 1997 a bareback horse bucked him off. Jim says, "He stuck my head in the dirt like a yard dart, head first, and I broke by neck." It was broke between C-6 and C-7 where the neck and shoulders connect. He was in traction for a week.

At the hospital he had no feeling from the neck down. He could not move his arms, fingers or legs. The doctors and nurses checked him out. They said, "You will be a quadriplegic." "No more bucking horses," was the report, "you won't even be able to walk again."

That is devastating news but the faith of God arose in his wife, Kay. She said, "Jim, right now, will you stand on God's Word with me? He focused his eyes toward her and said, "Yes, I will stand on God's Word right now."   Jesus is the Healer the Bible declares.

She then looked at the doctor (the Neurologist) and said, "I don't know who you are but I know you are not God!" He gave her his credentials. Kay replied, "It doesn't matter you are not God."

About thirty minutes later Jim raised his legs up and made a spurring motion like he was spurring a horse at a rodeo. Kay said, "What are you doing?" Jim replied, "I just wanted to know if they (his legs) would come up even." She got excited. The nurses said, "It's just a nerve reacting. Don't get excited."

Three or four days later they were in the room trying to calm him down. His arms were moving. He was slinging people away from him as they tried to hold him down. He said he needed to go to the restroom and he was trying to get up.

The doctors would walk by and say to Jim as he kept improving, "knock on wood."

Kay said, "Doctor, wood is dead. God isn't."

The doctor began proclaiming to the hospital staff, "This is a miracle."

The rest of the story is this. Jim did ride again about a year later in 1998 at the Stafford, Texas Rodeo. He won first place.

He won the Cowboy Professional Rodeo Association (CPRA) for the year and was crowned Champion Bareback Rider in 1998.

Another passion Jim has is to teach the next generation the sport he loves. He has taught young kids over the years to ride at Bareback Riding Schools. God told him, "Don't keep all that knowledge to yourself and take it to the grave."

He kept riding and winning for ten more years after the accident. Finally in 2007 after 37 years of riding bucking horses, he finished his career in the winner's circle. He was the 2007 CPRA and the 2007 UPRA (United Professional Rodeo Association) year-end Champion Bareback Rider.

He told his wife, "I'm done competing, but not done teaching."

He is now teaching the next generation the sport he loves at bareback riding schools.

Jim was a riding and walking miracle for ten more years after God healed his neck!

chapter

10

Give And It Shall Be Given

Give and it shall be given. Often we hear this quoted when talking about money. We do reap what we sow. Sow smiles, receive smiles; sow money, receive money; sow forgiveness, receive forgiveness; sow prayers, receive prayers.

When someone asks for prayer I sometimes ask another person to come and agree with me or to come do the praying or speak the blessing over the one who has a need.

I tell them, I want one of two kinds of people to pray. If you have had success in that area of need, or if you have this same need and are believing for a breakthrough, come up and pray over this person. If they have had a breakthrough and received a blessing of healing, or in a family situation, or a financial breakthrough, or got a job they needed etc, then their faith is built up in that area; they will pray in faith believing God will help this person in need as well.

If they have the same need the spiritual law and principal of "give and it shall be given" will begin to operate. Sometimes when people pray for others they both get the blessing they need from God. Pray for others - your answer/blessing will come to you also.

Recently in April 2007 my pastor, Cody Haynes, asked me to come up and pray for a friend I had rodeoed with twenty years earlier. His back was in pain. Earlier that morning I was speaking to my own back to line up with the Word of God. I had pain in my back and could not move fully and freely without it hurting. My movement was restricted. It was not intense pain but it hindered my activities. I was sitting in church and decided not to go up for prayer; I would just keep praying and speaking to the pain in my body in my own private time.

Well, at Pastor's request I did speak in faith to the man's body to line up with the Word of God. We called all pain out, and believed whatever should be tight, would be tight and whatever should be loose, would be loose!

By the time I got back to my chair I realized my pain was gone. My back was pain free, I could move in all directions and bend over with freedom and no pain. At this writing several months later I still have no pain and my back feels good.

I have seen others do the same thing and get a break-through. So if you have a need pray for someone else who has the same need. Give and it shall be given!

chapter

11
The Effecting of Miracles
The Bible Pattern For Miracles
How To Cause Miracles
How To See Miracles
How To Receive Miracles

Although God is "the Miracle Worker" we ourselves, often, have a part in the causing of miracles to happen.

In 1 Corinthians 12:4-10 we see that there are varieties of gifts, varieties of ministries, varieties of effects; they are all from the same and only One, the Holy Spirit. There are nine gifts of the Holy Spirit listed. One is the **effecting of miracles.**

1 Corinthians 12:4-11- (4) "Now there are varieties of gifts, but the same Spirit. (5) And there are varieties of ministries, and the same Lord. (6) There are varieties of effects but the same God who works all things in all persons. (7) But to each one is given the manifestation of the Spirit for the common good. (8) For to one is given the word of wisdom through the Spirit, and to another the word of knowledge according to the same Spirit; (9) to another faith by the same Spirit, and to another gifts of healing by the one Spirit, (10) and to another the effecting of miracles, and to another prophecy, and to another the distinguishing of spirits, to another various kinds of tongues, and to another the interpretation of tongues. (11) But one and the same Spirit works all these things, distributing to each one individually just as He wills."

So how do we effect or do something to cause a miracle?

The Bible has a pattern we can see that causes miracles to happen. This is not the only way but it is the way seen mostly, especially in the New Testament.

In the summer of 2007, I was meditating on something that I believe God was speaking to me. It was this: - "When they

25

prayed." "When they prayed, when they prayed." I said this slowly a few times for a day or two. Then I said, "I believe that's in the Bible." Well I should have known that pretty quickly since I had quoted a few verses with "when they prayed" in it for many years before I went out to minister at rodeos and elsewhere. So I turned to the passage and read it again although I have had it memorized for years.

Acts 4:29-31 and 33 (verse 29) "And now, Lord, take note of their threats, and grant that Your bond-servants may speak Your word with all confidence (or boldness), (30) while You extend Your hand to heal, and signs and wonders take place through the name of Your holy servant Jesus." (31) And <u>*when they had prayed*</u>*, the place where they had gathered together was shaken, and they were all filled with the Holy Spirit and began to speak the word of God with boldness."*

And (33) "And with great power the apostles were giving testimony to the resurrection of the Lord Jesus, and abundant grace was upon them all."

Who was this praying this prayer? Well it was John and Peter. They had been baptized in (filled with) the Holy Spirit days earlier in Chapter 2 of Acts on the Day of Pentecost. Yet here they are - praying to be filled again. There is one baptism in the Holy Ghost or Holy Spirit, but many fillings of the power of God in our lives.

So let's discover some things about miracles with the apostles. Look in the book of Acts in chapters 1-4 and Acts 7 plus in the life of Jesus. We will discover the Bible pattern for miracles.

In Acts 1:4-5 Jesus told the disciples to stay in Jerusalem and "wait for what the Father had promised." The promise was "...you shall be baptized in the Holy Spirit not many days from now." They needed the power of God in their lives. *Verse 8 "but you shall receive power when the Holy Spirit comes upon you and you shall be My witnesses...even to the remotest part of the earth."*

They needed this for the power and boldness to tell and show the world who Jesus is, the power He has and what He can do in a person's life.

We see they followed His instructions. Verses 13-15 tells that they went to the upper room along with Mary, the mother of Jesus and others, about 120 in all.

So in Acts 2 on the day of Pentecost 50 days after Jesus arose from the grave the Holy Spirit came in like a rushing wind. Tongues of fire rested on each one of them. *Verse 4 "And they were all filled with the Holy Spirit and began to speak with other tongues as the Spirit gave them utterance."* Then they went out to the streets with the gospel message. People from at least seventeen nations were listening and hearing them speak in their own native tongues.

The disciples told them that they had crucified the King of glory who is both "Lord and Christ - this was Jesus whom you crucified." In *verse 37, the people asked "Brethren, what shall we do?" Acts 2:38 "And Peter answered, 'Repent, and each of you be baptized in the name of Jesus Christ for the forgiveness of your sins; and you will receive the gift of the Holy Spirit.'"*

Result - about 3,000 souls were added that day and were baptized. So we see the power of God working in His people to convict people of their sins, causing them to repent and receive the greatest miracle - eternal life, salvation or deliverance from hell to heaven.

But other miracles are also available - the kind we need for life on earth.

In Acts 3 Peter and John, two of the ones who were in the upper room, were going to the temple to pray again. They were men of prayer. They had power because of prayer so they were ready to speak boldly. They saw a crippled man begging for money (he had been crippled for 40 years). So **Peter "spoke" to**

him in *verse 6 "But Peter said, 'I do not possess silver and gold, but what I do have I give to you, In the name of Jesus Christ the Nazarene - walk!'"* Verses 7-8 describes that immediately his feet and ankles straightened and with a leap he stood up and went to the temple to pray with Peter and John, leaping and praising God.

Now let's go back to Acts 4. They prayed to be filled again with the power of the Holy Spirit. This was Peter and John praying to be filled again although they had been filled with the Holy Spirit on the day of Pentecost a few days earlier. There is one baptism in the Holy Spirit, but many fillings.

We see in Luke 5 that Jesus after performing miracles with the large catch of fish for Simon Peter and the others, plus healing a man with leprosy, He then went off alone to pray.

Then He came out refreshed, refilled and performed more miracles including raising a paralyzed man to walk again.

So here it is - How to effect or cause a miracle! This is the Bible pattern we see.

1) First pray.

2) Then you will be filled afresh with the Holy Spirit and power.

3) Speak the blessings, speak the answer, speak the miracle.

4) Miracles happens.

Also look at the stories of Peter in Acts 9. He raised Aeneas who had been paralyzed and bedridden for eight years. He said in *verse 34 "Aeneas, Jesus Christ heals you; get up and make your bed.' And immediately he arose." (35) "And all who lived at Lydia and Sharon saw him, and they turned to the Lord."*

Next an amazing thing happened. Peter raised a person from the dead. Tabitha (also known as Dorcas), a disciple who was a well known woman in Joppa. She fell sick and died. The people there had great faith. Usually when someone dies people call the undertaker and make funeral plans. They called Peter instead and said, "Do not delay to come to us." There were people weeping in the upper room where she lay. *Verse 40 "But Peter sent them all out and knelt down and prayed, and turning to the body, he said, 'Tabitha, arise.' And she opened her eyes, and when she saw Peter, she sat up. (41) ...he presented her alive" And again we see in verse 42 "...and many believed in the Lord."*

So we see the same pattern here again. We know Peter was a man of prayer. First he prayed, God filled him with power obviously, then <u>he spoke</u> and said, "Arise." Then the miracle happened.

And on top of that many people received Jesus as Savior and Lord.

I have heard it called "power evangelism." When Jesus performed miracles, the people came; then He told them about the kingdom of God. When the disciples performed miracles crowds came, they presented the gospel of Jesus Christ and many were saved.

This is one outcome of miracles. But God performs miracles because He loves us. We need them, He has compassion on us and sometimes that is the only way we are going to get our breakthrough.

So remember, pray often, you will be filled afresh with the Holy Spirit, and then come out speaking boldly to the problems, situations, sicknesses, demons or whatever the need is and expect miracles! You will see them.

Prov. 18:21 "Death and life are in the power of your tongue..."

Speak life, speak blessing, speak healing, speak boldly, speak the Word, speak to the mountain, speak the answer - do it all in Jesus Name. You will get your miracle.

Have you ever received the greatest miracle - eternal life. If you died right now do have the assurance that you would go to heaven? You need to settle this issue. Is Jesus your Savior and Lord? He is the One who gives you eternal life. All who go to the

Father in Heaven must go through His Son, Jesus Christ. *John 14:6 "I am the way, and the truth, and the life; no one comes to the Father but through Me."*

Do you want God to forgive your sins, do you want a Savior, do you want eternal life, do you want to change your lifestyle, do you want the Holy Spirit to help you win in life? Pray this: God, I am a sinner, I need a Savior. Forgive my sins. Thank you for sending Jesus to shed His blood to wash away my sins and to die for me on the cross. I receive Jesus right now into my heart and life. Jesus you are now my Savior and Lord. Thank You for making a way for me to go to heaven and giving me eternal life. I can now call God my Father, heaven is now my home. Jesus, baptize me in the Holy Spirit for power to serve you. Holy Spirit help me live a life pleasing to my Father in heaven. In Jesus Name I pray Amen.

Now read your Bible everyday, pray everyday, get baptized in water, ask Jesus to baptize you (fill you to overfilling) in the Holy Spirit, meet with other believers often, and tell others about our Savior Jesus Christ.

Read Romans 3:10; 3:23; 5:8; 10:9-10, 13; Acts 1:8, Acts 2:38, Matthew 3:11, Luke 11:13, Acts 10:44-45, John 3:16, Matthew 28:18-20. Do what God says to do, how He says to do it, when He says to do it. Be a good witness to others, of the love of Jesus Christ and how He is active in your life.

Most of us have a lot of days on this earth after we receive salvation - your greatest miracle. Praise God, you are now on your way to heaven. Life still has a way of dealing us some battles and trials.

Some reading this may not need a miracle. You may need an attitude adjustment, a change in your work and sleep habits, a change in your diet or other things that will change your situation. But sometimes folks, there comes a time when nothing short of a miracle will get you through. Believe for a miracle - you usually get what you believe for. Miracles are still for today and available to you!

Paul said in *1 Cor. 4:19-20 "But I will come to you soon, if the Lord wills and I shall find out, not the words of those who are arrogant, but their power (20) For the kingdom of God does not consist in words,* but in power."

All authority is given to Jesus in heaven and earth. He gives that authority to us. Use that authority, speak blessings and watch God perform wonderful miracles.

How to Receive A Miracle!

Psalm 62:5 "My soul waits silently for God alone, for my expectation is from Him."

Begin to Believe for and expect miracles! Expect miracles in your life and in the lives of those you know and contact. Expect miracles for your nation and for the world. **Expect Blessings!**

How To Receive Miracles!

1. Stay prayed up. *Luke 5:16 "But He (Jesus) would often slip away to the wilderness to pray."* Acts Chapters 2, 3 and 4 "When they prayed" they were filled with the Holy Spirit, and spoke the word of God with boldness and saw signs wonders and miracles.

2. Be filled with the Holy Spirit. Ask Jesus to baptize you in the Holy Spirit and ask Him to continue to fill you to over flowing. Acts 1:8. *Ephesians 5:18 "...be filled with the Spirit."* When you spend time reading God's Word and praying, He will fill you with His Spirit, and you come out full of God, speaking the word of God boldly - signs and wonders and miracles will follow.

3. Keep speaking the word of God, keep speaking blessings, keep speaking life, speak miracles. *Proverbs 18:21 "Death and life are in the power of the tongue,..."*

Mark 11:23 "Truly I say to you, whoever says to the mountains, 'Be taken up and cast into the sea,' and does not doubt in his heart, but believes that what he says is going to happen, it shall be granted him." ("he shall have whatsoever he saith." in the KJV).

4. Walk by faith not by sight. *Hebrews 11:1 "Now faith is* the assurance of things hoped for, the conviction (evidence-KJV) of things not seen."

5. Expect Blessings! *Ps. 62:5 "...my expectation is from God."*

6. Believe the good report. Only two of the ten spies who spied out the promised land went in. They were Caleb and Joshua. They believed the good report that God gave them saying the promise land was theirs to take. The other ten saw the giants and walked in fear; they did not believe they could have the land so they never possessed it. See story in Numbers 13 and 14 and also the result in the book of Joshua. Joshua led all Israel into the promised land. And Caleb 45 years later at age 85 took the land he was promised and defeated and drove out the giants. (see Joshua 14:6-15 and 15:13-19).

7. Stay close to Jesus. The woman with the issue of blood pushed her way through the crowd until she touched the hem of Jesus' garment; then she got her miracle. The blood dried up. The hemorrhage she had for twelve years was healed.

8. Don't waver in unbelief because of circumstances. When Abraham was 65 years old God promised him a son by his wife, Sarah. He believed God and when he was 100 years old his wife, who was 90, gave birth to Isaac.

Romans 4:20-21 "...yet, with respect to the promise of God, he (Abraham) did not waver in unbelief but grew strong in faith, giving glory to God, (21) and being fully assured that what God had promised, He was able also to perform."

9. Keep believing the promises even when the time seems to have past for your blessing.

10. Remember - Miracles are for today! And miracles are for you. *Hebrews 13:8 "Jesus Christ is the same yesterday and today, yes, and forever."* God is no respecter of persons. He is not partial. Others have received miracles in this age - you can also.

So **(1) pray (2) be filled with the Holy Spirit (3) speak to your problem to go, speak the desired blessing to come (be specific) (4) miracles will happen.**

Miracles happen in other ways as well. God in His omnipotence will perform miracles at His will to accomplish His purpose, because of His compassion, when you find favor with Him, in answer to people crying out to Him and when He decides to because He is God.

11. Another key to your miracle is **prayers of agreement.** Believers come together, pray and stay in agreement for the breakthrough that is needed. *Matthew 18:19 "Again I say to you, that if two of you agree on earth about anything that they may ask, it shall be done for them by My Father who is in heaven."*

12. And then of course there is the plain and simple way of *Matthew 7:7* "**Ask** *and it shall be given to you..."*

13. In some cases of healing, **believers will lay hands on the sick and they will recover** (Mark16:17-18).

14. Also the sick can call for the elders who will anoint the person(s) with oil and the prayer of faith will raise them up. *James 5:13-15 "Is anyone among you suffering? Then he must pray. Is anyone cheerful? He is to sing praises. (14) Is anyone among you sick? Then he must call for the elders of the church and they are to pray over him, anointing him with oil in the name of the Lord; (15) and the prayer offered in faith will restore the one who is sick, and the Lord will raise him up, and if he has committed sins, they will be forgiven him."*

15. Use the authority God has given. Remember - all authority has been given to Jesus. Jesus gave that authority to us who believe. (See Mat. 10:1, Mat. 28:18-20, Luke 10:17-19). Miracles will happen for your betterment and for the glory of God.

16. Important! When believing for a miracle, say, "I receive it!"

17. Get in the atmosphere of healing. Go where people believe for and receive miracles. We see people receive miracles without ever being prayed for, or having blessings spoken over them when they are in a place where miracles are happening. Hang around people who believe in miracles. They will encourage you to beleive for miracles - miracles will and do happen. **Get your miracle!**

Miracle Blockers

Don't Block Your Miracles

1. Doubt and unbelief.

Matthew 13:58 "And Jesus did not do many miracles there because of their unbelief."

2. Lack of knowledge.

Hosea 4:6 "My people are destroyed for lack of knowledge..." (KJV)

3. Limiting God!

Psalm 78:41 "Yes, again and again they tempted God, and limited the Holy One of Israel.: (NKJ)

4. Believing that the time of miracles is past

Heb. 13:8 "Jesus Christ is the same yesterday, and today, yes, and forever." He is still doing what He has always done and will continue until His return and on into eternity. Man says the time of miracles is past - God does not say that. He still performs miracles.

5. Believing that "It may be for some but not for me."

God loves us all.

6. Bad confession - always speaking defeat instead of victory.

Stop telling God how big your problems are and start telling the devil and yourself and your problem how big your God is.

7. Believing that your miracle is just coincidence or fate and not giving glory and thanks to God for the miracle will block future miracles.

James 1:17 *"Every good thing given and every perfect gift is from above, coming down from the Father of lights, with whom there is no variation or shifting shadow. "*

8. Not expecting a miracle.

Psalm 62:5 "My soul, wait silently for God alone, for my expectation is from Him." (NKJ)

9. Believing your natural senses **more** than the Word and promises of God.

God gave us our five senses of seeing, hearing, taste, touch and smell. But to get a miracle you must believe God's Word and the power of Jesus Name more than what you see, hear, taste, touch or smell. Remember we are talking about miracles from God.

10. Not praying.

11. Not speaking the blessing.

12. Not staying close to Jesus.

13. Accepting your situation as being unchangeable (even by God).

14. Separating yourself from those who believe in miracles.

We are taught to come together to encourage one another.

15. Giving up. Quitting.

Stop believing for your miracles will block the miracle you need.

16. Not walking by faith.

Matthew 9 is the story of the woman who had a hemorrhage for twelve years. When she touched Jesus' cloak she was instantly healed. *Verse 22 says "But Jesus turning and seeing her said, 'Daughter, take courage; your faith has made you well.' And at once the woman was made well."* Also in Matthew 9 Jesus healed two men who were blind. *Verse 29-30 "Then He touched their eyes, saying, 'Be it done according to your faith. (30) And their eyes were opened..."*

Remember the greatest miracle is the salvation of your spirit and soul - to be given eternal life. We are saved by grace (unmerited favor) through faith. Other miracles come by faith as well. Jesus said, "Thy faith has saved you." We receive miracles by faith.

It is your faith in action when you speak a blessing and/or pray and ask for and seek a miracle before it happens.

17. Other things that block miracles include unforgiveness, disobedience to God, a lifestyle that blocks the miracle, an unrepentant heart and mind that does not want to change, unconfessed sin, wrong relationships, bad eating habits, bad sleeping habits, bad attitude, wrong teaching on miracles, learning to live with your situation and not expecting or even wanting a miracle, enjoying the attention you get (pity) because of your situation and because you did not get your miracle, becoming disgusted with God and not nurturing you love walk with Him, because you still don't have your miracle.

18. Blaming God for our troubles, problems, sickness, loneliness, instead of ourselves or the devil, thereby not expecting Him to change things since you blame Him for the situation anyway. You presume "It must be God's will." But the Bible declares in *John*

10:10 *"The devil comes only to steal, and kill, and destroy; I (Jesus) came that they might have life, and might have it abundantly."*

If it is killing, stealing and destroying, it isn't God. God is a good God. See III John 2 "Beloved, I pray that in all respects you may prosper and be in good health, just as your soul prospers. It goes on to say, they were walking in truth which pleases God. The truth will make you free (John 8:32). Love God and get your miracle! Then continue to love Him, serve Him, give Him thanks, honor and glory. Also you can use you miracle and your life to tell others about the goodness of Jesus. Psalm 34:8 "Oh, taste and see that the Lord is good; blessed is the man who trusts Him!"

19. Not believing in, understanding or knowing that angels are still on assignment to aid the children of God.

Angels are *"ministering spirits sent out to render service for those who will inherit salvation." See Hebrews 1:14.* Ask God to send out angels to help you and protect you and your family. When you speak the Word of God, angels listen and are *"hearkening to the voice of His Word." (Psalm 103:20) When angels hear us speak God's word they move into help us - we are God's mouth piece in the earth.*

20. Not doing what the Bible says to do -

The Bible instructs us to lay hands on the sick and they will recover.

The Bible instructs us to call for the elders of the church to anoint the sick person(s) with oil and pray so they will be healed.

The Bible instructs us to speak to the mountain to be cast into the sea.

The Bible instructs us to pray and believe.

The Bible instructs us to be filled with the Holy Spirit.

The Bible instructs us to speak the blessings into existence.

21. Not believing for a good report, but rather believing the evil report. Believe for a good report; you get what you believe for.

22. Whatever else you feel or know deep down inside that is blocking your miracle, deal with it and make the necessary change.

It would be better to love God now and into eternity without getting your miracle than to get your miracle and forget about God and not honor Him with your life. If God is dealing with you to make a change do it. Some people get their miracle and go off into or remain in a sinful lifestyle - they treat God and the miracle He did for them with no honor and respect. This blocks future miracles or they possibly lose the miracle they received.

DON'T BLOCK YOUR MIRACLES.

chapter
14

Stay Close To The Anointing
Stay Close To Miracles
Eyesight Restored

I was preaching at a Cowboy Church in Humble, Texas (near Houston) in about 1995 or 1996 I think.

God was doing wonderful work in the peoples' bodies. A lot of necks and backs were being healed.

They always roped steers after church on Sunday nights. A team roper came up to me as I ministered to the people. His elbow was in pain. Most were getting immediate healing and pain was leaving quickly. But when this roper walked up I said, "When you back into the box to rope later tonight the pain won't be gone, when you nod you head for the gate to open it will still hurt, when you raise your arm to rope the pain will still be there, but when you take your first swing of the rope the pain will go." When I saw him later he was grinning. He said, "It sure does feel good to rope without the pain."

Well the ministry for healing lasted about 30-45 minutes. Then a lady who had come with my sister came up to report this. She said, "I didn't come up for prayer I stood in the back of the room and watched. I could not see out of my right eye when I got here tonight. Now I can see clearly." I had told her to cover the eye that was good when she came in earlier. Now I instructed her to read with the eye that was healed. I had some t-shirts hanging on the wall across the room about forty feet away. She could see what was painted on the t-shirt and read out loud saying, "Just Rope It, Just Ride It, Just Spur It, Just Rodeo For Jesus!" She never was prayed for or spoken over yet she was close to the anointing of God and close to the miracles so she received her miracle - her eyesight! Praise God!

In Jones, Oklahoma in 2007 God was moving among His

people. Several received healing, pain was leaving, peace was restored during this two day meeting. When it was all over a lady I know came over to me. Almost everyone was gone. She said, "Ronnie I was so busy helping out (with things that needed to be done) I didn't come over for prayer, but I must have got close enough for God to bless me. The pain has left my ankle."

As I thought about what she said, the thought came to me. That's how it happened with the crowds when Jesus was among them. Multitudes were healed. Sometimes all were healed. They came expecting miracles and got close enough to His healing power and to the miraculous atmosphere it poured out onto the crowds.

I have been to meetings of a well-known minister who sees many miracles occur. People come expecting. People are healed and walk out of wheel chairs. They come off of oxygen breathing tubes as much as one to two hours before the minister even arrives at the coliseum or church. He says, "See I told you it is not me. It is Jesus. Don't look to me, look to Him." The atmosphere is alive with miracles and just getting close causes miracles for those in the crowd.

What am I telling you? If you need a miracle get around people who believe in miracles.

When I first went into the ministry, I printed our first newsletter with our mission, visions and expectations. I drove to Houston, Texas where I attended the World Convention at Lakewood Church hosted by Pastor John Osteen. In one service I experienced an amazing move of God. As he preached he stopped to pray over one lady's elbow. Then he stopped preaching and said, "I am going to raise my hand and move it across the crowd. If you need a miracle, receive it as I move my hand across the room." It was amazing. Miracles begin happening all over the building. One man received a creative miracle. He did not have a bicep muscle when he had come in but now the muscle was there. A man from Africa who sold all the furniture at his Bible School to pay for his trip to America received his eyesight. He was to have it operated on when he returned to Africa. No need for that now. I talked to that man personally, after the meeting. People gave reports of healing and miracles for about thirty minutes; there were more but they shut the meeting down and let the people go so they could prepare for the next session. As I was sitting in the middle of the church I could hear bones cracking, people making sounds, praising God. It was quite an experience. That encouraged me - miracles are for today. Miracles happen!

The interesting thing was only one woman was personally ministered to. The rest were close enough to the miracle working power of God. Stay close to miracles. You will get your miracle.

Bobby Davis, of Rodeo Cowboys For Jesus Ministries in Bryan, TX, attended a ministers' conference in Round Rock, TX. in the spring of 2009. I was teaching on healing that day. Bobby came up to be spoken over for healing of back pain, while I was speaking over others and seeing God heal them. Bobby was patiently waiting and watching, I turned to him and said, "What do you need?" He responded, "Nothing, the pain is gone." I smiled and said, "Well, go sit back down." Bobby had come forward by faith and got his blessing and left pain free. Bobby got close to the anointing and received his healing. Then I continued to see God heal others.

chapter

15

Because Of The Blood...

- **Torn Groin Muscled Healed**

- **Shoulder Pops! Back In**

- **No Need For Oxygen Tank**

Cody Haynes is the pastor of Faith Christian Cowboy Church of Johnson City, Texas. He also breeds, raises and supplies bucking bulls at rodeos and bull riding events. Cody says, "My bulls are all about Jesus."

He does a lot of one on one ministry, and often he has a cowboy church service at the events he goes to.

He has seen a lot of miracles among the cowboys.

He prayed over Jacob Payton, a young cowboy, one night at a rodeo who had a pulled groin muscle. He was not able to ride his horse and rope and tie calves or ride bulls because of this injury. God touched him. The pain left. The next morning Jacob attended church where Cody is the pastor. He began attending regularly. His relationship with Christ began to grow. He became excited about Jesus. In just a few weeks Jacob called Pastor Cody and said, "I am going to miss church Sunday, I think I need to go pray for a man I know who is in the hospital." The man was paralyzed from the waist down. The doctors' report was that he may not walk again. Jacob asked Cody what he should read over him. Cody responded, "Read Isaiah 53 over him." When Jacob read the Scriptures over him his legs jumped off the bed. It scared Jacob and he ran out of the room. The doctor came into check it out and said it was just his nerves causing a reaction. But the next day he was walking and left the hospital in three days. He still walks and is in good health. A few months later he drove big machinery and worked on the church parking lot.

God touched Jacob. He received his healing, then began

serving God and ministering to others. The Bible says "freely you received, freely give." His lifestyle changed. He loves God and loves people and brings them to know Jesus as Savior, Lord, Healer and the Best Friend you will ever have.

A bull rider's shoulder popped out of joint at a rodeo in Bulverde, Texas in November 2007. The EMS (Emergency Medical Service) said, We are not going to try to put it back in. You need to go to the hospital." The bull rider is a Christian and believed in healing. Cody went over to him and by faith spoke healing. Cody said, "I can't put it back in, but Jesus can. But I will give you a little tip. Put your elbow back close to your side and it will pop back in." The bull rider kept saying, "Thank you Jesus! Thank you Jesus!" The shoulder popped! back in! Cody said, "It wasn't my faith - it was the cowboy's faith."

One more quick report in closing, is that one day Cody prayed over a lady out in the middle of a cow pasture. She was on an oxygen tank to aid her breathing. She left that pasture breathing on her own with no need for the oxygen tank.

Often God shows Cody the pain in a person's body before they tell him they have it. It is called a "word of knowledge." (See 1 Corinthians 12:8) Sometimes God shows Cody an area of sin or bondage in their life that is blocking their blessings. He prays against all assignments of the devil in their life and sees victory come from God. He has a great understanding and knowledge that the Blood of Jesus has paid for our healing, is the path to miracles, frees us from sin and the results of sin. Because Cody honors the blood of Jesus he sees many miracles.

chapter
16

Ringbone And Fear

I spoke at Tomball Cowboy Church (now known as Saddle Creek Church) in Tomball, Texas in the mid 1990's. The service was over and we had dinner on the grounds. This church met in the alley of a horse stables. It eventually grew from 40 people to 400 or more and they bought another building. In those early days people were coming to receive Jesus Christ at most of the services. They began to grow in Christ and change their lifestyles. They began to trust God more and more in their daily lives, in their businesses and with their animals.

One of the horse trainers there asked me to pray over his horse. He rode expensive horses and this was his full time occupation. The horse had ringbone, a calcium deposit just above the hoof that was causing him some trouble. I went toward the horse to laid hands on him and the trainer said, "Be careful, he's kind of spooky." I said, "We'll just pray the fear out too."

I laid hands on the horse and spoke the Word of God over him such as, "Father your Word says 'they shall lay hands on the sick and they shall recover.'" I also spoke peace over the horse. I don't remember exactly what I said, but we prayed in agreement and I went off to my dinner.

The horse was tied to an electric horse walker going round in circles with about four or five other horses. About fifteen minutes after we prayed something spooked the horses. All but one were pulling back on the lead ropes. The one we prayed over, who was normally nervous and spooky anyway was just standing there calm with his head down relaxed. I just smiled and kept eating.

A few weeks later, the horse trainer told me the horse was healed, he was solid and healthy and said, "I sold him for good profit."

chapter

17

Lord Of The Wind, The Clouds, The Rain

Jesus said that He did nothing or said anything unless He saw His Father do it. You take on the actions of the one you respect and spend time with. We are told in 1John 4:17 "...as He (Jesus) is, so also are we in the world." Now the context of that verse was to abide in love. To abide in love is to abide in God. God is love and God is powerful. Love keeps your motives right. When you abide in Jesus, you take on His nature. You spend time with Him and you begin to act like Him.

A fierce wind and storm caused the waves of the sea to cover the boat Jesus and His disciples were in. What did Jesus do? He rebuked the wind. He said, "Hush, be still." And the wind died down and it became perfectly calm. (See the stories in Matthew 8:23-27 and Mark 4:35-44). We see what Jesus did. What are we to do?

Rain Clouds Part And Go Around

The rodeo was about to begin. The rodeo announcer, John Mack, was up in the announcer's booth and called to me saying, "Ronnie come up and say the opening prayer." I went up in the announcers stand. We were having a short visit before the rodeo. Then he looked up and said, "Ronnie, look at those clouds!" I looked and what I saw was some huge very dark clouds being blown right toward the rodeo arena and at the announcers stand where we were. The wind had begun to blow a little harder and the temperature was cooling down quickly. The rain clouds would be over us it seemed in a matter of a few minutes, perhaps ten minutes or so. It was now about 7:10 p.m. The rodeo started at 7:30 p.m. In the natural prospects for a wet rodeo looked very real. But when I looked and saw the black clouds, the first thing I thought and said was, "I command you to part and go around this arena in Jesus name." I did not scream. I did feel a strong surge of faith arise in me, I just simply spoke to the clouds. Then I continued to visit with John Mack. In just a few minutes he said, "Ronnie, look!" as he pointed to the clouds. The clouds parted in the middle and began to go around on both sides of the arena. By rodeo time we were dry, the wind died down, the clouds were on either side of the arena. We had a nice dry arena and good weather for the rodeo. During the bull riding, the last event, it began to sprinkle a little. When the last bull was bucked and the rodeo was over it began to rain.

No Rain - Sixteen Years At Rodeo Schools And Bible Camps

My faith to believe God to hold off the rain grew over the years at the Rodeo Schools and Bible Camps we sponsored for sixteen years.

Many of those years, our faith was tested often, the night before, or the very morning of the first day of the school. The forecast was for rain to come, clouds hovered over us and around us. We had prayed and believed God for good schools and for lives to be changed.

Several of those schools we rode and roped in some mud but never did it rain during the day at instruction time. (One time it rained during the trophy ride off on the last day during the bull riding, after the instruction time was over and the school was ending).

It would sometimes rain at night during the Bible Study, but never when we needed the outdoor arena.

At that time, myself and those in the ministry helping at the camp were not speaking to the wind, clouds and rain. We were simply asking God for His favor. Proverbs 3:3-4 says we can "find favor with God."

Those were the years that I did college ministry. The college kids' faith was growing. Several of them are now in full time ministry as pastors, traveling evangelists and church workers. Some years we would use the outdoor arena in the day and the indoor arena at night for supper and Bible study. One year we were in the indoor arena and began to hear the rain on the steel metal roof. Some of the students at the school who were from out of town said, "Well, I guess we will have to use the indoor arena tomorrow." The college bunch that had been involved in helping sponsor the Rodeo School/Bible Camp for a few years laughed and said, "It's not going to rain tomorrow." Well, God honored their faith and it was dry during the day as we continued to teach and ride horses and bulls. The outdoor arena was a much better arena set up and that is the one we preferred to use. We tried the indoor arena one or two days during the years. But we believed for favor with God to be able to use the outdoor arena.

The students learned rodeo skills they needed and many competed at rodeos for years into the future. Many kids received Jesus as their Savior and Lord. Their lives were forever changed.

Lord, I Believe You Will Keep The Rain Off This School

One year that sticks in my mind is this; the first day there was no rain but clouds were near. That night as I was studying the

Bible and preparing a message for the students, I heard the pitter patter of rain on my roof. Suddenly I remembered that I left my rodeo gear at the arena. I jumped in my car and drove five miles to the arena. There lay my bag open with the equipment - bareback rigging, chaps, spurs, etc. - uncovered.

It was just a light sprinkle. I gathered my things and started the drive back home north of Huntsville, Texas on I-45. I was almost home when I said, "Lord there are some things I can believe You for. I believe You will keep the rain off this school." About five minutes later I pulled into my garage at home and opened the door to the living room. The television was on and the weatherman had a picture of the state of Texas on the screen. He said, "It is raining everywhere in Texas." Every county in the state was shown to have clouds and rain over it. I just walked on by and went back to another room to finish the Bible lesson.

Well to my knowledge it rained everywhere in Texas the next couple of days. It rained in Walker County where we lived and held the Rodeo School and Bible Camp. It rained all around us, but it did not rain on the arena we were using. Praise God! We had a good school and enjoyed the presence of God and the blessing of God in the weather.

Several years later we sponsored a Rodeo School and Bible Camp in Boerne, Texas. The final ride off for trophies was about to begin. Rain clouds had blown in and were hovering over the arena. I remembered how God had been gracious and blessed us for so many years. I said, "Lord I don't want to get cocky (prideful) about all these rain stories, but could You do it again. Would You hold the rain off?"

One of the instructors was at the other camp the year it rained everywhere in the county except at the arena we were using. His memory was more vivid than mine. He said, "Hey, Ronnie, do you remember the year it rained all around that arena, but not on us." I responded, "I don't remember seeing it that clearly but yeah, I remember." Praise God! We finished the afternoon with good weather; God did do it again.

Rain And Wind Stops At Pro Rodeo

It was Saturday night, the final performance of the Helotes, Texas P.R.C.A. Rodeo. Everything was going well but during the Barrel Race it began to sprinkle and a light rain started. I was standing behind the bucking chutes next to a rodeo committeeman I knew. The bulls were already loaded for the final event of the rodeo.

The committeeman said to me, "I had hoped the rain would hold off until the performance was over." I looked at him and said, "Well He says ask and it shall be given. Let's ask God to stop the rain." He said, "Okay." I prayed, "God will you please hold the rain off until after the rodeo? In Jesus name, Amen." The rain stopped almost immediately. The wind died down. The rodeo committeeman looked at me and smiled. The barrel racing event was soon over, they bucked about ten bulls, the rodeo was over, then shortly after it began to rain. "Ask and it shall be given."

A year or two later my children and I went to the Santa Fe, New Mexico P.R.C.A. Rodeo. In the middle of the rodeo the dust was blowing and a storm was brewing. Most of the rodeo contestants went over to be under the bleachers for cover. I was standing next to a security guard and told him the story about what happened at the Helotes, Texas rodeo. I said, "Let's just do it again. Let's ask God to stop the wind and rain." I asked and the wind died down in a few minutes. The cowboys came back to the bucking chutes, took their equipment out to get ready to ride and the rodeo went off smoothly in nice weather. We never even told the cowboys what we did. We just smiled at the goodness of God as

He honored our faith and our prayer.

Sometimes we just go ahead and ride in the rain, the wind and the mud. It's time to get tough and "cowboy up" as they say. But often we can tap into the favor of God and experience the good weather we desire.

So keep praying, keep asking, speak boldly to the wind and the rain. That is what Jesus did. We are to do as He did.

... Same Rodeo - Several Years Later...

I went to the Helotes, Texas P.R.C.A. Rodeo again several years later, in 2010 to minister and hold Cowboy Church services for the contestants in their dressing area. (This was a few years after the above story).

The clouds began to hover over the arena. It looked like it would rain the first performance. I saw the same committeeman who heard me pray when the rain stopped at the last performance a few years earlier. We looked at each other after we looked up at the clouds. I said, "Remember when the rain stopped the last time we were together?" He said, "I sure do." We grinned at each other and I said, "Well, let's do it again." I prayed, "Father, would you hold the rain off the rodeo this year." It cleared up pretty quickly and we had three days of sunshine and cool nights for the rodeo performances.

Rain Stops At Del Rio, Texas

In May 2008 I was preaching at the George Paul Memorial Bull Riding in Del Rio, TX. I had shared how God had split the clouds at the Boerne, Texas Rodeo so they went around the arena. We had just spoken to pain to leave bodies. People were healed.

Nine people prayed to receive Jesus as their Savior. Of course that is the greatest miracle, for a soul headed toward hell to be delivered and headed to heaven. About 50 or more of the 100 plus crowd prayed for Jesus to baptize them in the Holy Spirit for power to serve God more boldly. Some of the bull riders were helping pack the sound system and other things to get them out of the way for the spectators who would be sitting in the bleachers that we had just used for Cowboy Church. It began to sprinkle small rain drops, there was cloud cover as far as you could see.

I said, "Rain Stop." I had just been teaching about the signs, wonders, miracles and the power and promises we have in the New Testament through Jesus Christ. The rain stopped immediately!

We all began to smile and laugh as we finished packing.

The bull riding went on for the next few hours in a nice, cool, cloud covered afternoon. It is usually very hot and sunny each year at this bull riding. Thank you Lord.

Almighty God Lord Of The Winds, The Clouds, The Rain

18 Miraculously Healed Horses

by Layna Kight - WNFR Barrel Racer and Horse Trainer

I wanted to share a couple of the healings God has done for my husband, Hoby, and myself in behalf of our animals. God showed me that in Genesis 1:26-27 that it was my responsibility to receive by faith (the healing provision already given to us through Jesus) over the animals entrusted to my husband and me. God has been faithful to deliver many healings to us and our animals over the years. Here are two that have always seemed to minister to others.

First, we owned a thoroughbred filly that we purchased for re-sell as a race horse. To preview those horses before they are sold they breeze 1/8 or 1/4 mile before potential buyers on a specific day, and then they are sold through public auction one day after this performance.

Therefore, to prepare these horses they usually have a pre-breeze to prepare them before the real breeze day. During this breeze-prep this filly pulled her suspensory, she was unable to put any weight on that leg and was diagnosed by attending veterinarians.

So my husband and I got in the word of God concerning healing that night. Later that night we went to the barn and prayed over her, led her limping out of her stall and confessed over her that by Jesus stripes she had been healed. We then had three days until her real breeze show. During this time we didn't discuss her condition, but continued to hand walk her and confess that by Jesus stripes she had been healed. Each night we left worship music playing in her stall and by the third day her healing was manifest. She breezed at the top ten percent of all the horses in the sale, was sold and remained perfectly sound. Praise God!

Next we had a client's race horse in our training program. He was in his stall saddled awaiting his turn to train for the day. While in his stall he got his mouth hooked on a piece of his equipment called a yoke which was around his chest and neck. Once he was in a bind, he flipped over and we believe he broke his neck. He could not lift his head or move his body. We approached his stall immediately, prayed over him with the laying on of hands and then confessed that by Jesus' stripes he was healed. Later that afternoon he showed great signs of improvement and the next day his body had responded to God's word and he was completely whole again. The next day he went back to training and never had any complications.

Editor's comment:

Healing is a finished work - it's up to us to feed our spirit on the Word in order to receive it and walk in faith. Jesus is the Name above all names. He is above all pain, sickness, brokenness, heartaches, fear, depression, lack of any kind, every evil spirit and any other name that is named.

Pain is a name. God gave Jesus the name above all names. (See Philippians 2:9-10 and Ephesians 1:19-20). So Jesus' Name is above pain. Jesus took stripes on His body before the cross for peace and for our healing. (Is. 53 and Mat. 8:16-17) He took a stripe for cancer, He took a stripe for heart disease, He took a stripe for pain. **"So, in Jesus' name - Pain you must go. You tell it to go." The pain will leave your body.**

Matthew 4:23-24 Jesus was going throughout all Galilee, teaching in their synagogues and proclaiming the gospel of the kingdom, and healing every kind of disease and every kind of sickness among the people. (24) The news about Him spread throughout all Syria; and they brought to Him all who were ill, those suffering with various diseases and pains, demoniacs, epileptics, paralytics; and He healed them.

Not Breathing, No Pulse...

"Bull Riding!" PRCA Texas Circuit Finals Rodeo. The rodeo announcer stirs the crowd to excitement.

I was sitting in the grandstands watching my friends ride. We had prayed before the rodeo together. Now the battle was on.

A well known bull rider, Blu Bryant, who had been a Runner-up to the World Champion Bull Rider was about to ride. I had performed his wedding ceremony a year before. I could see his wife and mother sitting a few seats away.

Blu was an accomplished bull rider. He had been riding since he was young boy before his teen years. He was no stranger to pain. Broken bones, among other things had caused him to sit out for months more than once. But he healed up and came back riding good every time.

Back to the action. Blu's bull turned out and spun right out of the gate and slammed Blu to the ground. He did not move. Instantly he was knocked out. The crowd went silent immediately.

His wife, Alley, and mother, Bonnie, and a friend of mine, Ron Conatser, who is a cowboy preacher hurried down stairs to the arena floor to check on Blu and pray over him. They knew it was bad. They usually would not have gone into the arena. They have seen a lot of bad wrecks where the cowboy would eventually get up and walk away. This one was different. The EMS and sports medicine people quickly attended to the situation.

I stayed in my seat and stretched out my hand toward him and prayed.

Then as I watched, his body jump off the arena floor in a jerky motion and he fell back into the dirt motionless. It reminded me of the movie, "Rocky II," when the Russian boxer floored Apollo Creed, the former heavy-weight boxing champion. In the movie, his body did a quick jerk off the floor and then he laid still and died. When I saw that I jumped out of my seat as I thought, "I better go down there."

I walked over to Blu. He was flat on his back - motionless. His eyes were rolled into the back of his head. I laid hands on him and prayed. I heard the rodeo announcer say, "Ronnie Christian, our cowboy preacher, is praying over him" as he encouraged the audience to do the same.

I got up and walked over to the bucking chutes to give the paramedics room to work. His wife was standing there. She is a registered nurse. She knew it was bad. She said, "Ronnie - go pray over him." I said, "I just did." She said frantically, "Go pray again." So I went back to him and prayed again. A lot of people were praying all around that rodeo arena.

They took him out on a stretcher to the ambulance and on to the emergency room at the hospital.

When I got to the hospital there were several cowboys and others there to check on Blu. His mom, Bonnie, said that he was fighting the doctors and nurses and they had to tie him down.

She had brought Blu up in a Christian home. Blu was a strong witness to his peers about Jesus. With the peace of God in her voice and a smile on her face she said to me, "Oh, I took care of this a long time ago." With all the prayers and entrusting Blu to God she knew he was in the good hands of the Father. She had peace that comes from trusting and resting in God.

In about an hour or so his wife, mom and myself went into the intensive care unit into Blu's room. There was Blu, totally out. We prayed over him the prayer of faith and the peace of God came on us. I said, "He is just getting a good nights sleep," and we left him there. God was not through with Blu yet; He had more things for him to do.

Sure enough at the next nights performance of the rodeo, Blu came walking in. His eyes were still a bit glazed over and he was not in condition to ride his next bull but he looked good considering what he went through the night before.

He healed quickly and rode more bulls for the next couple of years. Now for the rest of the story. Several years later we were teaching at a Rodeo School and Bible Camp in Huntsville, Texas in June 2008. Blu was the bull riding instructor. We were standing in the rodeo and arena and he said, "I'm a walking miracle. Remember that wreck in Waco, Texas at the Circuit Finals." I said, "I remember. Was that a miracle?" He said, "I wasn't breathing and I had no pulse. I was dead." I said, "I don't remember that part." He said, "When you're not breathing and you don't have a pulse you're dead." It's a miracle I'm here."

Praise God for giving him the breath of life back. They had one child, a boy, named Sterling, at the time of the wreck. Now they have a daughter, Cheyenne, also.

He loves to teach the next generation of bull riders about the sport and about his Savior and Healer Jesus Christ.

Matthew 10:7-8 "And as you go, preach, saying, 'The kingdom of heaven is at hand.' (8) Heal the sick, raise the dead, cleanse the lepers, cast out demons; freely you received, freely give."

20
Jesus -
The Name Above All Names
Pain Is A Name

Jesus is the Name above all names. He is above all pain, sickness, brokenness, heartaches, fear, depression, lack of any kind, every evil spirit and any other name that is named.

Pain is a name. God gave Jesus the name above all names. (See Philippians 2:9-10 and Ephes. 1:19-20). So Jesus' name is above pain. Jesus took stripes on His body before the cross for our peace and for our healing. (Is. 53 and I Peter 2:24) He took a stripe for cancer, He took a stripe for heart disease, He took a stripe for pain. **"So, in Jesus' name - Pain you must go. You tell it to go." The pain will leave your body.**

Matthew 4:23-24 Jesus was going throughout all Galilee, teaching in their synagogues and proclaiming the gospel of the kingdom, and healing every kind of disease and every kind of sickness among the people. (24) The news about Him spread throughout all Syria; and they brought to Him all who were ill, those suffering with various diseases and pains, demoniacs, epileptics, paralytics; and He healed them.

See in verse 24 it says He healed pain. I was holding a Cowboy Church service at the rodeo in Del Rio, Texas on the 4th of July weekend in 2008. I said as I closed the service, #1) settle your eternal destiny - receive Jesus as your Savior; #2) Ask Jesus to baptize you in the Holy Spirit and fire - the fire of God will burn out the junk and tendencies to sin and fire you up to serve Him. He will fill you to overfilling with the Holy Spirit, and give you power to be a bold witness for Jesus and give you power over the enemy - the devil and demons and over your own flesh; #3) if you have pain in your body let me know.

As soon as I released everyone in a final prayer an older

bull rider came straight to me. He said, "Ronnie, I have pain all over my body." I told him, "Pain is a name and Jesus is the name above all names. That means it's above pain." Then I put my hand on his shoulder and he bowed his head thinking I was about to pray over him. I said, "Don't bow your head, look at me! Jesus took stripes for our healing." Then I illustrated someone with a whip giving lashes. Each time my hand went down I would name something. "One stripe was for cancer, one stripe was for heart disease, one stripe was for pain I told him."

So he is now looking at me, opened eyed. I put my hand on the back of his neck and asked, "Is it your back?" He answered, "Yes." I ran my hand down his back from his neck to his waist and said, "Pain you have to go! In Jesus Name," and I took my hand off his back and took a step back. Immediately he said excitedly, "How did you do that? How did you do that?" I laughed and answered, "I didn't do anything, Jesus did." Then immediately I said, " That is not true; I did do something. I did what Jesus did and I did what He told us to do. I called the rodeo producer over and a couple of others who were still close by at the end of the Cowboy Church service. He told those standing there watching, "When his hand left my back, all the pain left."

The man who was healed told me before we spoke to the pain to leave that he had excepted Jesus as his Savior about three years earlier. He said, "I live for Jesus now." He was now 49 years of age. Most bull riders retire in their late 20's or mid 30's. He told me that he began riding again last year at 48 years of age, 16 years after he had retired from riding bulls. He said, "It's like riding a bicycle. It came right back to me. I won the Senior Pro Bull Riding last year in my area."

He is still enjoying what he likes to do, riding bulls. This time around he is serving his Savior, Jesus, and being a light to others, plus now he knows Jesus is the Healer as well.

At this point in the ministry I see people are open to the power of God. Pain is leaving bodies everywhere I go.

The next week we were in Jacksonville, Texas at the P.R.C.A. Rodeo. Pain left a bull riders shoulders after I instructed all the people at Cowboy Church in the grandstands to point to him and say "Pain - go! In Jesus Name." Another cowboy who rode bareback horses and saddle broncs had pain in his legs, the pain left when I spoke it.

A barrel racer on the front row said, "I have pain in my neck and my shoulder." I walked over and laid hands on her neck and called the pain out in Jesus' Name. I walked back over to conclude the service then I looked at her and said, "All the pain didn't go yet, did it? She said, "No." I said, "It will before you walk out of that gate to leave. We closed the service and she was about to pass by me as she was leaving to get ready to compete. I stopped her and asked her, "Did you notice how Jesus spoke healing over people and they were healed instantly." She nodded yes. I said, "But do you remember the time Jesus Himself spoke to a blind man to receive his sight, then Jesus asked 'What do you see?' The man replied, 'I see men walking like trees.' And Jesus spoke to the eyes again. The man's eyesight was completely restored." She remembered the story. So I put my hands on her neck again and spoke to the pain to go as I moved her head slowly to the left and slowly to the right. (I think I said as I often do when joints are involved, "Whatever should be loose - be loose and whatever should be tight - be tight.") She smiled a smile of relief as the pain left. Then I touched her shoulder and said, Pain go from this shoulder too in Jesus Name." She competed pain free that night! As I left the Jacksonville, Texas Rodeo I began praising God, not about me or how he was using me recently, but that the people **are so open** to the full gospel, to healing, to salvation and to the baptism in the Holy Spirit and fire. They are open not only to the fruit

61

of the Spirit; love, joy, peace, etc. (in Gal. 5:22-23) but also the power gifts including praying in tongues and interpretation of tongues, prophecy, gifts of healing, miracles...(see I Cor. 12:8-10). I saw the barrel racer at a rodeo in Bryan, Texas the following week and asked her how she was feeling. She smiled and said, "I'm still feeling good." I said, "Praise God."

It would take up many pages if I told you all the stories of pain leaving bodies recently. Sometimes I relay their stories to people I see at different places such as at my mechanics garage or the post office. They get excited, it builds their faith. Then when they tell me about their pain, I speak to the pain to go and in Jesus' name it goes.

We are just having fun serving God.

<u>Eternal Pain of sin leaves.</u>

Remember once again that Jesus is the same today as when He walked the earth. He is still saving people from hell and taking them to heaven, He is still baptizing people in the Holy Spirit and fire (Acts 1:5, Acts 1:8, Acts 8, Acts 10, Acts 19) and empowering them to serve God <u>and</u> He still is healing people's infirmities and taking away their pain.

Also, I mentioned to the people at the Del Rio, Texas Rodeo Cowboy Church service that **#1)** they should settle their eternal destiny. For two days I had done a lot of one on one personal ministry. I had taught what the word of God said, counseled, listened, talked, prayed and encouraged several contestants and others who were there with them. We had a late supper on Saturday night, compliments of the rodeo committee.

I didn't leave until 12:30 a.m. Sunday. It had been a good weekend. The ministry was over or so I thought. I drove through the parking lot to pick up my seventeen year old son, Brandon, who was visiting with his friends. About 20-25 young people were gathered around playing loud music. Most were drinking beer but remained civil. This was the younger bunch having their own after the rodeo party.

One young man, about 21-23 years old I guess, walked over to my R.V. and said, "Hey Ronnie I want to get on of those Cowboy Bibles but I don't have any money." I said, "They are free." Go inside into the back of the R.V. and get one. Get one of the books I wrote also. It is called *"Hang On To Your Hope!"* He got them out of a box. I'm sitting in the driver's seat. He is standing right behind me. I asked him if he had ever asked Jesus to be His Savior. I said, "Have your ears ever heard your mouth say, 'I am a sinner and I need a Savior.'" He said, "No." We had developed a friendly relationship over the past two years. He came to the Cowboy Church services, and to the prayer time behind the bucking chutes before the rodeos. He said, "I have been to churches but they always seem to talk down at people. I like the way you talk." I said, "Well some relate to me and some don't." Then I asked him, "Do you want to pray and receive Jesus." "yes, he answered." We prayed together. He asked God to forgive him of his sins and accepted what Jesus did for him on the cross when he died and shed His blood to wash away his sin. He said, "I receive Jesus as my Savior and the Lord of my life. Thank you for eternal life." Jesus took the pain of sin out of his heart.

I looked up at him. There he was a new baby Christian standing there with the book I wrote and a Cowboy Bible in one hand and the two beers he had when we first started talking in the other. My thought was, "Some religious folks could not handle that (seeing him with the beer and praying). My next thought was "Jesus could care less about those two beers at this moment. God looks at the heart, man looks at the outward appearance."

So I just smiled and we said "Good-by and God Bless you." Praise God! It was a great way to end a weekend of ministry at the rodeo

One last reminder - Pain is a name. Jesus is the name above all names. It is above pain. So pain has to go. So I say to

your pain, "PAIN GO!" In Jesus Name. Now you tell it to go!

Scripture References:
Philippians 2:9-10 "For this reason also, God highly exalted Him, and bestowed on Him the name which is above every name, (10) so that at the name of Jesus EVERY KNEE WILL BOW, of those who are in heaven and on earth and under the earth."

Ephesians 1:18-20 "I pray that the eyes of your heart may be enlightened, so that you will know what is the hope of His calling, what are the riches of the glory of His inheritance in the saints. (19) And what is the surpassing greatness of His power toward us who believe. These are in accordance with the working of the strength of His might (20) which He brought about in Christ, when He raised Him from the dead and seated Him at His right hand in the heavenly places. (21) far above all rule and authority and power and dominion, and every name that is named, not only in this age but also in the one to come"

Matthew 4:23-24 "Jesus was going throughout all Galilee, teaching in their synagogues and proclaiming the gospel of the kingdom, and healing every kind of disease and every kind of sickness among the people. (24) The news about Him spread throughout all Syria; and they brought to Him all who were ill, those suffering with various diseases and pains, demoniacs, epileptics, paralytics; and He healed them."

I Peter 2:24 "and He Himself bore our sins in His body on the cross, so that we might die to sin and live to righteousness; for by His wounds (stripes) you were healed."

Nine fruits of the Holy Spirit.
Galatians 5:22-23 "But the fruit of the Spirit is love, joy, peace, patience, kindness, goodness, faithfulness, (23) gentleness, self-control; against such things there is no law."

Nine power gifts of the Holy Spirit.
I Corinthians 12:8-10 "For to one is given the word of wisdom through the Spirit, and to another the word of knowledge according to the same Spirit; (9) to another faith by the same Spirit, and to another gifts of healing by the one Spirit, (10) and to another the effecting of miracles, and to another prophecy, and to another the distinguishing of spirits, to another various kinds of tongues, and to another the interpretation of tongues.

A parting thought. The gift of healing and the gift of miracles is still working in people's lives. Receive it for your own life and those around you. Believe for miracles.

Healed of Cancel - PBR Church

A lady came up to me for prayer at the end of the Professional Bull Riders (PBR) Finals Cowboy Church service in Las Vegas. I think it was in1999. She said she had cancer. She looked a little weak but was fairly healthy looking. Anyway, we prayed over her and she left.

I had no further contact with her until the PBR Cowboy Church service one year later. She spoke with me after the service and relayed to me the following, "You prayed for me last year .I had cancer but now I am healed." That was her report and she left. I do not know what happened during that year. All I know is the name of Jesus is above cancer and this lady was blessed by the Healer, Jesus Christ. What a blessing it is to tap into His love and healing power.

21

Prayer Of Agreement
Heals Bucking Horse

On another occasion with the college kids at Sam Houston State University I was preaching a message on faith. This again was at the weekly Bible Study and Buck Out. I would preach and teach the word of God for about a half hour then some of those attending would go to the arena and practice their rodeo event. In this case it was bareback riding.

The rule was, if you got there for the opening prayer the practice was free. If you were late you had to pay to help buy feed for the horses.

One night a young college boy brought his roping horse to try out as a bucking horse. He would throw a fit and start bucking at times. He was tired of trying to work the buck out of him or maybe tired of getting bucked off. So he thought the horse may have a better future as a bucking horse.

We bucked him out that night and sure enough he bucked hard and we were all yelling and clapping. But then immediately the horse pulled up lame. He pulled or tore something in his rear leg. He could not straighten his leg out or put his foot on the ground.

Now remember, I had just preached a message on faith in God. With God nothing is impossible. Faith believes God for something you cannot see, but know God will take care of it. Jesus would say, "With God nothing is impossible"; "Your faith has healed you." "Your faith has saved you."

To be honest when I saw that crippled horse my faith went down. The Bible says in 2 Cor. 5:7 "for we walk by faith not by sight." But my sight took over.

However the word of God had gone forth that night. It had

been implanted into the souls and spirits of those college kids.

Two of them said, "Let's go lay hands on that horse and pray for him." So the two of them, myself and a few others gathered around that horse. We laid hands on him and God healed him instantly.

A person on another horse led him around the arena. He was not limping. He was sound and good to go. So we released him and he required no further attention to his leg.

The boy, David McMahon, who owned him grew up to became a well-known PRCA rodeo announcer. He took the horse to a rodeo stock contractor who eventually bought him. A few years later I was preaching at a Cowboy Church service at the year end CPRA (Cowboy Professional Rodeo Association) Finals in Bay City, Texas.

McMahon who previously owned the bucking horse sang at the church service. After church he said, "Remember that horse of mine we bucked out. He was voted the Bucking Horse of the Year in the CPRA." I guess he was more suited for bucking than roping.

I'm glad those young kids at that college arena that night exercised their faith. When they said, "Let's lay hands on him and pray," my faith arose and joined theirs. Also a few others joined in. Walking by faith encourages others to have faith.

God not only healed that horse, but he became a Champion Bucking Horse.

ACL And MCL Healed

A bull rider was sitting in pain after the PRCA Rodeo in Huntsville, Texas in 2007. He was talking to the wife of a well known bull rider. She and her husband are spirit-filled Christians. They know the power of God is real for today. The two of them had been encouraging the young bull rider to grow in his walk with God. They had exposed him to anointing the sick with oil and laying hands on the sick for healing. He was explaining to her that he just hurt his knee very badly. He said, "I think that I tore my ACL (anterior cruciate ligament)." I was next to them listening.

Then I laid my hands on his knee. I said, "I command this body to line up with the word of God. I call the ligaments, tendons, muscles, nerve endings and every cell and fiber in this body to line up with the word of God." I told him, "Pain is a name. The name of Jesus is above all pain." Then I said, "Pain you have to go in Jesus' name."

Cowboy Church in the bleachers was about to start in about five to ten minutes. I said, "I have to go and do a church service. Listen, believe for a good report. You usually get what you believe for." I hurriedly walked away to preach at the Cowboy Church service.

A few minutes later, just before I began the service, another spirit-filled bull rider came to church smiling and reported, "Hey, all the pain is gone, his knee is healed.

After Cowboy Church we all went to eat at the cowboy campground on the rodeo grounds. I sat across from the now healed bull rider. He said, "These guys took me to their church in Mississippi; I didn't grow up in a church like that. To be honest, I though anointing the sick with oil and praying for the sick was a little strange." He kicked his foot out and back, bending his knee a few times and with a big smile said, "But it don't hurt anymore."

Another cowboy touched by God. He left understanding that God's power to heal is real and Jesus is the Healer in todays world.

A few months later the same bull rider was stomped on by a bull at the PRCA Rodeo in Los Fresnos, Texas in February 2008. The way he was responding I was sure he had broken a rib. He ended up behind the bucking chutes in my arms. He was spitting up blood and I thought he probably or possibly punctured a lung. He was sick at his stomach and could not breathe very well. I prayed over him and spoke life to his body then I helped carry him to the emergency medics on the grounds of the rodeo.

He did not get an instant miracle and they surmised the same thing, his lung might be punctured. They felt he needed to go to the hospital for a check-up. His friends, the same bull rider and his wife that were with him at the Huntsville, TX rodeo were with him. They went to the hospital. I called them on my cell phone a couple of hours later. The report was about the same. Two weeks later I found out that he left the hospital that night and was able to compete in the bull riding the following week at a college rodeo.

Another cowboy who is a bareback rider was getting ready to ride at the PRCA Rodeo in Lufkin, Texas in April 2008. I asked "How have you been doing? He replied, "I tore my MCL (medial collateral ligament). I laid off a few weeks. I have a knee brace on." I felt the knee brace through his jeans pants. Then once again I spoke healing. I said pretty much the same thing as I had said to the bull rider, "Pain you have to go - In Jesus name."

After he rode, he jumped on the bucking chute that I was standing behind, grinned real big and said, "Thanks!" I asked, "No pain?" - The report, "No pain."

23

Bucking Horses Calm Down

At rodeos there is a lot of excitement and noise. Sometimes the horses like the cowboys get very nervous and anxious just before they buck in the arena. In the bucking chute some horses begin to paw, kick, bite and sling their head, sweat, shake and rear up. It is a place where cowboys and horses can get hurt.

I had heard that animals can have an evil spirit. Remember the demon that Jesus cast out of the man. The spirits went into the pigs and they ran over a cliff. (see Luke 8:26-39).

I realized the horses that were acting so bad were not crazy, although some of them do seem to have a mean streak and are just plain mad. But we tend to think those causing all the ruckus are crazy.

I noticed that these horses were in fear. The "spirit of fear" was on them. I began to shake their mane and pet them on the neck as we have done for years. But I also began to speak to the spirit of fear. I would get close to the horse and say, "Your spirit of fear, go!" The horse sometimes would still act badly and so I would say, "You got to go. Fear go in Jesus Name!" They would settle down a bit and then I would get close to them, look them in the eye and say, "Now receive peace." They might snort and act uneasy for a bit. Then again I would calmly say, "Peace in Jesus Name, receive peace." I may repeat it in some cases more times than others.

The horses would calm down so the rider could get in the chute (or if already in the chute, get in a good position to compete), get ready and go on to ride.

Some horses the moment I speak and touch them settle down immediately.

The horses that have a record of fighting in the bucking chute will have a "neck rope" on them. (A neck rope goes around the neck of the horse and the chute gate to control the horse and keep it from injury and from injuring the rider. It is released when the gate opens). When the horses calm down we usually leave the rope on. But after speaking to the fear and releasing peace the horse is now calm and is not pulling against the rope and trying to rear up and smash the cowboy.

I mentioned this at a rodeo Cowboy Church service one year, about 2006, at Bay City, Texas. About an hour later one of the cowboys, (and his dad) who attended church service were getting a bareback horse ready to ride. The horse was squatting low in the chute; he was shaking and sweating. He obviously was in fear. The dad looked at me. I spoke to the spirit of fear to leave. Immediately the horse stopped shaking, he stood up. The cowboy was able to get his gear on the horse and sit on him in the chute with no problem. His dad looked at me again and said, "We are going to find you the next time we have another chute fighting horse." Of course they don't need me. They just need to use their authority in Jesus Name.

A horse was rearing up in the chute with bareback rider, Luis Escudera, at a rodeo that same year in Pueblo, Colorado. His hand was already in the bareback rigging and the neck rope was on the horse. I walked slowly toward the bucking chute to help. I did not want to spook the horse. But as I got closer, Luis, reached through the chute, grabbed my wrist and pulled my hand to touch the horse's neck. Immediately the horse stood still, the cowboy was able to get into position and nod for the gate to open. He left the chute with no problem and made a good ride.

I realize and the cowboys realize that these are unbroken bucking horses that are high strung animals. They are set on "go." Sometimes a person has to "cowboy up" (go in a tough situation) and take the horse when he is not in the best ideal position. But I have seen many, many horses calm down when the spirit of fear goes and we speak the peace of Jesus to them.

chapter
24

From Broken Neck To WNFR

(As reported by Lance Crump - WNFR Bareback Rider)

I walked out of my house one morning; my one-year old son was asleep in the house. I had flown in from a rodeo for the weekly Cowboy Church Service and Buck Out that I had every Tuesday at my arena for local youth and adults alike. At the time, I was eighth in the PRCA Bareback World Standings, in the lead to win a Dodge truck in the Dodge Rodeo Series and only a few wins out of leading the world standings. Things were good; God was blessing my family and me. I had a beautiful Christian wife that fully supported everything I did and a beautiful baby boy!

As I was loading bulls we had used in the Buck Out the night before, one of the bulls jumped one of the panels I was using to load them in the trailer and hit me from behind. All the weight of the bull and the panel came crashing down on the back of my neck. When I came to (regained composure and was conscious of my surroundings) I could not move my hands, but I could hear myself saying, "Help Me Jesus" as I lay there in the pen of six or more bulls. I crawled under the fence and to my house to check on my son. I called my wife who was at work. She came and we went to Dallas to the doctor. After x-rays and scans, they told us I had fractured the C-6 vertebra in my neck and that I would need to go to a Specialist. They put me in a straight brace for ten days and told me not to move wrong or I would risk being paralyzed.

I had a Youth Rodeo to preach at in seven days. With the Lord's help, I preached. At the end of the service the kids who had been attending our buck outs came up, laid hands on me, and prayed for healing.

Later that night sitting in my chair in my living room I was hurting so bad I begin praying and asking God if it was His will for me to have a broken neck, be paralyzed, miss the WNFR (Wrangle National Finals Rodeo), lose my home and everything I have worked for. If so, I am willing to accept that, but I do not believe that is Your will. I KNOW, You can heal me and allow me to go to the WNFR and tell people of Your healing powers and this miracle in my life. I asked my wife to lay her hands on me. Sitting in my living room with my hands held high in the air to God we begin to pray. As we prayed, I felt God's healing touch as it went to the injury in my neck with the literal healing taking place as only He can do.

Three days later, I went back to the same specialist and after new x-rays he told me that it was an old injury. I said, "You told me ten days ago that it may require surgery and that I had a risk of being paralyzed." He said he could not explain it, but there was a calcified bone around the injury. I shared with him about Jesus and the prayer of healing. He said, "Go do what you do. That was mid-September 1997. I had slipped from eighth in the world to fifteenth. By the end of October, I had only one qualifying rodeo left to help me hold the number fifteen slot to qualify for the WNFR. I flew to Casper, Wyoming in a "had-to-win" situation to make the WNFR. With the first place win I accomplished the Lord and I were WNFR bound. Praise God!

At the finals in the fourth go round, I was interviewed on ESPN television and told the world how the Lord healed me.

Every day we must learn to ask God His will for our life, accept it, and leave the RESULTS up to HIM. When you know Jesus is the Healer, you can expect and receive your miracle easier.

chapter
25

Champion Cow Dog
Raised From The Dead

(As told by Merle Newton to author)

Merle and Sandy Newton operate Crystal Rose Cow Dog College at Red Bluff, California. They train cow dogs to work with horses as they sort and move cattle in a timed obstacle competition course.

Merle had an exceptionally good young prospect he was training. He named the young dog, Smarty.

As he was getting ready for his first competition Merle learned what the Bible had to say about first fruits giving. First fruits always goes to God then He will bless the future fruit. It's not the ten percent tithe we usually hear about but it's the whole thing.

Well Smarty won at his first showing in 2006. It was a small show and it paid $300.00. So Merle gave (seeded) all the winnings to Cowboy Church International (aka Pro Rodeo Ministries) whose founder is cowboy preacher, Coy Huffman.

At a practice session shortly after the event Merle and Sandy were continuing Smarty's training. As Merle watched he was thinking, "What next? Should I seed all of Smarty's winning or ten percent to the Lord?"

About that time, the young dog ran into the back of a herd of cows. Several cows kicked him and Smarty flopped over and laid still. Sandy checked him. He was not breathing. She shouted, "He's dead!" Now these people are ranchers. They know when an animal is dead. Merle went over and laid hands on Smarty and prayed over him saying, "No, no I got plans for you. Lord this can't be. Can you help little Smarty?" Immediately Smarty jumped up, totally alive and totally healed.

Then Smarty went right back to working cows. Usually

after a dog gets kicked that hard they will stay back a little ways from the cows. But Smarty went right back to working as he had before the incident. Merle said, "Lord, he's Yours now."

All the winnings (that year) of Smarty's now would go to the Lord's work. Winnings of $10,000 came in that year. All winnings went to promote the gospel.

Merle says that some will say, "Well he was just knocked out. When doubt like that comes God reminds him about Smarty's chronic cough. When the dog got the cough Merle said, "God you didn't raise this dog from the dead to have his happen. It has to get out of here." He coughed one time. Merle responded, "That will do." He never coughed again.

Then in 2008 at Sealy, Texas at a Cowboy Ministers Conference, Smarty got a bad ear infection. The veterinarian could not cure it. There was a hole in the eardrum. About ten cowboy ministers laid hands on and prayed over the dog. Merle and Smarty flew back to California in a jet plane. The ear got worse.

The veterinarian at home in California looked at the ear and, "Nothing is wrong." And added, "I did not heal him and I am not charging you for my services."

When doubt comes in about whether that Smarty was really raised from the dead, God speaks to Merle and says, "What about the cough? What about the ear?"

Merle knows God did raise his dog from the dead. That's hard for skeptical brains to believe. But today Merle is enjoying working Smarty and showing him at the competitions.

Miracles still happen - even to our animals.

chapter
26

The Revelation

Have you ever had a pain in your body but did not know what it was caused from? You don't know what it is; you just know it doesn't belong there? Something is wrong, but you don't know what it is? And truthfully you are not sure you want to know. You just know something is not right.

Well I had one of those in about 2002 or 2003. When I drove to rodeos to minister, after about three or four hours, a sharp pain would hit my side. It was just under my bottom rib and just above my pant belt line. Usually it was on the right side but sometimes it would move to the left side.

I didn't want to tell anybody. I was still trying to figure it out. What is this? How should I pray? If I call someone for a prayer of agreement what will I call it? On a daily basis it never bothered me at all, only when I sat and drove for three to four hours.

I finally mentioned it to one cowboy preacher friend of mine. He said, It sounds like the hernia I had one time." I said, "No that isn't it." So I did not say anything to anyone else.

We will come back to this story in a few moments for the ending.

I had this drainage in my throat for a few days. It was nothing major, but at night I could not sleep very well. I would prop my head up on my pillows to try to get more comfortable. This went on for about three days.

It's not like I had cancer or some bad disease or sickness. But it was aggravating and uncomfortable.

As I was driving my van on one of my errands for the ministry this thought hit me, "Lord, it cost Your Son too much on the cross for me to have this drainage in my throat." <u>God</u> <u>gave</u> <u>me</u> <u>a</u> <u>"fresh</u> <u>revelation"</u> (and reminder) <u>that</u> <u>Jesus</u> <u>took</u> <u>stripes</u> <u>for</u> <u>my</u> <u>healing</u> (before the cross).

I never had another night's drainage and discomfort in my chest and throat. It was completely healed.

A few weeks later I was at a church in Kerrville, Texas. A man came over to me and asked me to pray over the bread or the wine when we partook of the Lord's Supper. That church had recently rented the whole movie theater to view the movie, "The Passion of Christ." It was a movie that very graphically depicted the gruesomeness of the stripes Jesus took for our healing, of the beating he endured, and of the crucifixion itself. But when it was all done Jesus said, "It is finished!"

He finished what God sent Him to do. Mainly He finished the work that we needed for our sins to be forgiven, for us to be reconciled to God, for us to have eternal life, for heaven to be our home.

He also finished the work for us to have peace, healed hearts, healed minds and healed bodies. (See Isaiah 53, 1 Peter 2:24-25)

When it was time for me to speak I took the bread representing the broken body of Jesus. I prayed something like this as the people listened, "Father, it cost your Son too much on the cross and before the cross for these people to go around sick, disgusted, broke, down hearted. Thank you for taking care of all our needs. Give us a fresh revelation of what you did on the cross for us. I thank you. In Jesus Name, Amen." We took communion. I left, not knowing God had done a work in my body.

Now back to the pain in my side. It was no longer there.

A few days later I drove to minister at a rodeo. It was about five or six hours away from my home. After three or four hours I noticed the pain in my side was not there. The little bubble I could feel with my finger was gone. I was totally pain free, completely healed. It has been several years now. I still do not now what caused the pain or why I could feel a little bubble of some sort on my inside, but it no longer exists. The Bible says in Isaiah 41:11-12 you will look for your enemies and they be as nothing (King James Version says, "they that war against thee shall be as nothing, and as a thing of naught"). The New King James says they will be as nothing, you shall seek them and not find them - those who contended with you. Those who war against you shall be as nothing, as a <u>non-existent</u> <u>thing</u>."

What happened in this story is this - I got a fresh revelation of what Jesus paid for us to be healed spirit, soul and body. He paid the full price for our full healing. Say, "I receive it!."

Expect miracles because of what Jesus did for us!

The Greatest Miracle Is Yours

To know that your sins are forgiven and eternal life is yours is the greatest miracle. Only God can remove all your sins to the place of total forgiveness, forgetting them and not holding your sin against you. You can be clean before God and man.

The Blood of Jesus washes sins away. Jesus is the way to the Father in Heaven. "Jesus said to him, 'I am the way, and the truth, and the life; no one comes to the Father but through Me'". (John 14:6) You are invited and welcome to come to Him.

If you know that there is sin in your life and you need to confess your sin and ask for forgiveness, that is the Holy Spirit leading you to God. Listen to Him. He wants you to repent-to change your mind, your heart, your direction and turn from sin to Jesus.

Jesus died on the cross and took your sins. He also took stripes on His back for you to have peace, for your healing and the miracles you need. You can have the love of God inside of you. God loves you very much and He wants you to be with Him. You can love yourself and others. You are very precious and valuable to God the Father. Receive Jesus and the love of God today. The Holy Spirit will come to live in you and be your Helper, Comforter and Guide who will lead you into all truth. You will have the fruit of the Spirit - love, joy, peace, patience, kindness, goodness, faithfulness, gentleness, self- control (Galatians 5:22-23). You will still have temptations and battles and challenges but God will be with you now in your battles so you can win and walk in victory.

First off, settle your eternal destiny. Pray this - Dear God, I am a sinner, I need a Savior. I ask You to forgive me. I ask Jesus to come into my heart. I believe that You died on the cross for

me to wash away my sin. I receive You right now and confess Jesus as my Savior and the Lord, the Master of my life. I believe you rose again and I will too. Heaven is now my home. So I say, "I am saved, I have eternal life, Jesus is my Lord." In Jesus Name Amen.

Now, get baptized in water. See Matthew 28:18-20, Acts 2:38. Read the Bible everyday, pray everyday and meet with other believers often - get connected with a good church and have a Pastor speaking life from the word of God into your life. Find a church full of the love and power of God flowing in the people. It will be a place of learning and encouragement. Also it will be a place where you can serve and prepare to use the gifts God has given you to help others in the world to know Jesus and with their daily life.

Ask Jesus to baptize (immerse) you (fill you to overfilling) in the Holy Spirit. The Holy Spirit will give you power to be the person God wants you to be. He will lead, guide and help you. The Holy Spirit will give you power to be a witness - for Jesus. The Holy Spirit will give you power over your enemy, Satan, and his demons. The Holy Spirit will help you pray. The Holy Spirit will keep you in the love of God.

Read Luke 10:17-20; Jude 20-21; Romans 8:28; Acts 4:29-31,33.

Acts 1:8 "but you will receive power when the Holy Spirit has come upon you; and you shall be My witnesses both in Jerusalem, and in all Judea and Samaria, and even to the remotest part of the earth."

Acts 10:44-48 (44) While Peter was still speaking these words, the Holy Spirit fell upon all those who were listening to the message. (45) All the circumcised believers who came with Peter were amazed, because the gift of the Holy Spirit had been poured out on the Gentiles also. (46) For they were hearing them speaking with tongues and exalting God. Then Peter answered, (47) "Surely no one can refuse the water for these to be baptized who have received the Holy Spirit just as we did, can he?" (48) And he ordered them to be baptized in the name of Jesus Christ. Then they asked him to stay on for a few days.

Luke 3:16 "John answered and said to them all, "As for me, I baptize you with water; but One is coming who is mightier than I, and I am not fit to untie the thong of His sandals; He will baptize you with the Holy Spirit and fire."

Pray. Jesus I ask you to baptize me in the Holy Spirit and fire. Burn out everything that is not pleasing to you and fire me up to serve you. Fill me with the power of God to be a bold witness for you, to overcome the enemy, to see signs, wonders and miracles for your glory. In Jesus Name, Amen.

Now open your mouth and begin to pray. You will pray in your native tongue and also in an unknown tongue. This is praying in the Spirit; the Bible says we are to pray and sing with our mind and we are to pray and sing with the sprit. (see I Cor. 14-15. You are speaking mysteries, the Holy Spirit is speaking in and through you. You will be edified (built up) empowered to serve God and make a difference in the world for the good. Go - preach the gospel. You will see others come to Jesus, be healed, change their lifestyle for the good and enjoying the love, joy and peace of God. It will happen in your life and in the lives of those you reach for Jesus, you will see the miracles of God!

chapter
28
It Is A Miracle? You Decide.

We have seen the gift of healing working for many years. I believe the gift of miracles is now working also on a more regular basis. Is it a miracle when these things happen? You decide.

Isn't it interesting that the people who are healed and the things we see don't happen until we pray, or get into agreement over the situation, or speak to the situation to change?

We speak to rain clouds; then they go around the arena and it does not rain on the rodeo grounds until the rodeo is over.

We speak to pain; the pain does not leave until we speak. Is that a miracle? You decide.

People and horses are healed; it does not happen until we anoint them with oil and pray and/or speak healing over them. Is that a miracle? You decide.

Jesus said in John 14:12 that we would do works that He did. Peter and John prayed that they would speak the word of God with boldness and that Jesus would extend His hand to heal, and signs and wonders would take place through Jesus' name. They received great power to witness about Jesus, and signs and wonders, miracles and healings did take place through them.

Scripture references:
John 14:12 ""Truly, truly, I say to you, he who believes in Me, the works that I do, he will do also; and greater works than these he will do; because I go to the Father. "

Acts 4:29-31, 33 "And now, Lord, take note of their threats, and grant that Your bond-servants may speak Your word with all confi-

dence, (30) while You extend Your hand to heal, and signs and wonders take place through the name of Your holy servant Jesus. (31) And when they had prayed, the place where they had gathered together was shaken, and they were all filled with the Holy Spirit and began to speak the word of God with boldness. (33) And with great power the apostles were giving testimony to the resurrection of the Lord Jesus, and abundant grace was upon them all."

The gift of miracles is listed here:

I Corinthians 12:1-11 Now concerning spiritual gifts, brethren, I do not want you to be unaware.

(2) You know that when you were pagans, you were led astray to the mute idols, however you were led. (3) Therefore I make known to you that no one speaking by the Spirit of God says, "Jesus is accursed"; and no one can say, "Jesus is Lord," except by the Holy Spirit. (4) Now there are varieties of gifts, but the same Spirit. (5) And there are varieties of ministries, and the same Lord. (6) There are varieties of effects, but the same God who works all things in all persons. (7) But to each one is given the manifestation of the Spirit for the common good. (8) For to one is given the word of wisdom through the Spirit, and to another the word of knowledge according to the same Spirit; (9) to another faith by the same Spirit, and to another gifts of healing by the one Spirit, (10) and to another the effecting of miracles, and to another prophecy, and to another the distinguishing of spirits, to another various kinds of tongues, and to another the interpretation of tongues. (11) But one and the same Spirit works all these things, distributing to each one individually just as He wills.

Mark 16:20 "And they went out and preached everywhere, while the Lord worked with them, and confirmed the Word by the signs that followed." ("And they promptly reported all these instructions to Peter and his companions. And after that, Jesus Himself sent out through them from east to west the sacred and imperishable proclamation of eternal salvation." - this paragraph is found in some later manuscripts).

Remember God is no respecter of persons. He is not partial. He loves all of us. We can put ourselves in a position of blessings though while others will not. Continue to draw near to God and He will draw near to you. Keep your heart pure. Keep trusting God. Don't limit God. Believe for and expect miracles in your life and those around you. Listen to the Holy Spirit - do <u>what</u> He says to do, <u>when</u> He says to do it and <u>how</u> He says to do it.

Jesus is the Healer and Miracle worker! He still does what He always has done.

Psalm 105:1 - Oh, give thanks to the Lord! Call upon His name; make known His deeds among the peoples! (2) Sing to Him, Sing psalms to Him; talk of all His wondrous works! (3) Glory in His holy name, let the hearts of those rejoice who seek the Lord!(4) Seek the Lord and His strength; seek his face forever more! (5) Remember, His marvelous works which He has done, His wonders, and the judgments of His mouth.

John 20:30 Many other signs therefore Jesus also performed in the presence of the disciples, which are not written in this book; (31) but these have been written that you may believe that Jesus is the Christ, the Son of God; and that believing you may have life in His name.

Hebrews 13:8 Jesus Christ is the same yesterday and today, yes, and forever.

Lord, This Has Got To Work For Me Too!

Report by and about the author, Ronnie Christian

The Bareback Riding event is what I competed in for 26 years, from age 14 to 40. I got on hundreds of horses - about 1,000 I guess. I was blessed to stay healthy and injury free most of the time. (I also entered the Bull Riding for 14 years plus entered the Steer Wrestling for three years and Saddle Bronc Riding at college rodeos for two years.)

In 2001, at age 50, I got on six bucking horses after a ten year layoff.

Then in 2009 at age 58, I decided to get on a few more. I feel good, I exercise five to six days a week. I help with two or three bareback riding schools a year and get on the bareback horse spurring dummy at the schools. Also at my house I get on a spurring dummy we had made for my son, Brandon. I did not need to ride to prove anything; it does not define who I am or what kind of bareback rider I am or was. I just had the desire to ride. My head is still in the sport. I don't have to ride - I'm just glad I feel good enough to ride - praise God. At 58 years of age that may not me a miracle but it is definitely a blessing.

I went to Del Rio, Texas to a rodeo July 3-4th. The first night I got on an exhibition bareback horse. I wanted to check my equipment and myself. The next night - Saturday, July 4th I was entered in the Bareback Riding event. The announcer said, "This man started riding in 1965 at age 14. That was 44 years ago!"

As I rode I made an error - just the opposite of how I teach. I came off the horse and hung up (my hand was hung in the rigging). I ran along side the horse like we teach trying to free my hand but I lost my footing. Then I was under the horse. He stepped on my legs in five places and I was out and free quickly. I knew my right leg had a serious injury but I walked out of the arena. My knee would feel like it would almost come out of joint in one particular position I get be in. It was swollen and sore.

Of course I spoke life and healing over it. I had others do the same.

A few weeks later, I went to a rodeo to minister in Monte Vista, Colorado. There was a Chiropractor with a table set up in a room by the bucking chutes. I thought, "I'm going to ask him what I did to my leg." He checked me out thoroughly. I laid on my back with my knees up. He sat on my right foot, then pulled my leg below my knee in towards him and back away again. There was some slippage we could feel in my knee. It was loose. Then he had me to cross my right foot over to my left knee. He grabbed my ankle and said, "Hold your leg in a bent position." I could not do it. He would pulled the leg straight out.

The report was - "You are not swelling or badly bruised - what you did was tore your ACL (anterior cruciate ligament). The rest of your muscle group around it is in good condition so you can still function." Then he gave me a laser gun to put on it and some other sore spots I had.

That night I woke up about 3 a.m. and got out of bed. As I sat in a comfortable recliner chair, I laid my hands on my knee and said, "I call everything in this body to line up with the word of God. I call everything that should be tight to be tight; I call every-thing that should be loose to be loose. *I Peter 2:24 says, "'by His (Jesus) stripes we were healed.' Matthew 8:17 says, 'He (Jesus) took our infirmities and carried our diseases.' Psalm 27:1 'The Lord is the strength of my life.'"*

As I thought of miracles we have seen in others I then said, "Lord this has got to work for me too." After that I went back to bed to sleep.

The next morning, Sunday, I took my sound system to the

rodeo for them to use at a Cowboy Church service. Then I went to speak at the Feed Store Family Training Center in Monte Vista. About one half of the 200 attending received ministry to be healed of wounded spirits. About seven received Jesus as Saviors. Several had pain leave their bodies instantly, miraculously.

And then I said to the people there, "The Bible says, 'freely you received, freely give.'" It's your turn. Get in agreement with me for my knee to be healed. I spoke life and healing as a I did when I was alone the night before. The people stretched their hands and their faith toward me.

I knew it was not 100% healed but something was different. After church it was time to go back to the rodeo for the Sunday afternoon performance. I said to myself, "I'm going to get that Chiropractor to check my knee again." So when I got to the rodeo I used his laser again. Next I asked him to check me out. He asked me to do a few moves and checked my movements and my strength. He kept saying, "Not bad - not bad." Then I asked, "Check my knee again like you did yesterday." So I crossed my right leg over my left knee again. This time when he tied to pull it straight I could hold until he applied a lot more pressure to straighten it. His words to me were, "Now that's a testimony. It's not the same." I asked him what type of exercises I could do to strengthen it. I said, "I will be diligent to exercise and do what I can do in the natural. I'll ask God to put his super on it and I'll get supernatural."

The next week and I was at the rodeo in Eagle, Colorado. Another Chiropractor was set up to work on the contestants behind the bucking chutes. I told him about my ACL and the report I got the weekend before. He knew the other Chiropractor. We visited a few days at each performance. On the last night of the rodeo, I asked him to check my knee. After checking it over thoroughly he said to me with a smile, "If it was torn, it isn't now. What you have is a stretched MCL (medial collateral ligament). Keep doing your exercises and it will tighten up.

The horse had also kicked my ankles and they were swollen so much. I could not get my boots on for four weeks so I wore comfortable slip-on shoes and sandals. But on this day, my 58th birthday present, on August 1, 2009, was this - I could get my boots back on again. My knee was much better. This was four weeks after my injury began. I continued to do exercises.

At six weeks my leg felt very good - probably it was 90-95% healed. It actually felt good enough that I could ride again if I had chosen to.

Eight weeks after the injury, my leg, ankles, knee felt very good. I could do all activities with no restraint. I would say I was at 98% since I had a little swelling and a very small pain in a certain position I would get into. At nine weeks I told a rodeo contestant that I felt 98-99%, but then I realized it felt 100% and my knee feels great now. It is totally healed.

So by the Chiropractors reports - My ligament was torn one day and the next it was different. The next weekend the report was, it is not torn at all. A miracle! Thank you Jesus!

In the Friday night ride, July 3, 2009, the night before my injury I felt some muscle spasms in my back and neck after my first ride. I had some cowboys to speak healing over me. I said, "I have been praying and speaking over you guys for 30 years. Now it's your turn to speak healing over me." I was pretty stiff. The next day before my Saturday night ride I went swimming. I spoke to my body to be healed, in Jesus Name. Then I said, "Lord this has got to work for me too!" When it was time to ride Saturday night I had no muscle spasms or soreness in my back and neck. And I have not had any since that night.

The Saturday night bareback riding injury produced another more serious challenge.

I remembered what I said so I said it again for this injury -

"Lord this has got to work for me too!"
And it did - I am healed!
Praise God!

And It Has To Work For You Too

The Lord does not love the people whose miracles are reported in this book any more than He does anyone who is reading this book. He is not "a respecter of persons." He is not partial.

So believe for your miracles.

Prayers, speaking miracles, laying hands on the sick, anointing the sick with oil, prayers of agreement, the Blood of Jesus, the Name of Jesus, Scriptures in the Bible and more are all given to us for healing and other needed miracles. So believe for good reports. *"Jesus is the same..." Hebrews 13:8.*

He is still the Miracle Worker.

Mark 16:20 "And they went out and preached everywhere, while the Lord worked with them, and confirmed the word by the signs that followed."

Believe for your miracle
and you will get your miracle too!

TRAIL TO HEAVEN

Romans 3:10 - There is none righteous, not even one.

Romans 3:23 - For all have sinned and fall short of the glory of God.

Romans 5:8 - But God demonstrates His own love toward us, in that while we were yet sinners, Christ died for us.

Romans 6:23 - For the wages of sin is death, but the free gift of God is eternal life in Christ Jesus our Lord.

Romans 10:8-10 - (8) But what does it say? The word is near you, in your mouth and in your heart - that is, the word of faith which we are preaching, (9) that if you confess with your mouth Jesus as Lord, and believe in your heart that God raised Him from the dead, you shall be saved; (10) for with the heart man believes, resulting in righteousness, and with the mouth he confesses, resulting in salvation.

Romans 10:13 - for, "Whoever will call on the name of the Lord will be saved." You can know you are saved, your sins are forgiven and you have a home in heaven, eternal life with God forever.

John 3:16 - For God so loved the world, that He gave His only begotten Son, that whoever believes in Him should not perish, but have eternal life.

Revelation 3:20 (Jesus said) "Behold, I stand at the door and knock; if anyone hears My voice and opens the door, I will come into him, and will dine with him, and he with Me. Receive Jesus today by praying a prayer like this:

Dear God, I am sorry for my sins. I ask you to forgive me of all my sins; I turn away from sin and I turn to you. I accept Jesus as my Savior and my Lord right now. Thank you Jesus for dying on the cross and shedding your blood for me to wash my sins away. I confess right now that Jesus, You are my Lord. Thank you for giving me a home in Heaven. Baptize me in the Holy Spirit. Dear Holy Spirit, I ask you to guide me all the days of my life. Thank you God that I can call you my Father and thank you for giving me eternal life. I praise you! In Jesus name, I pray.

Turn to the book of John and read it through.

(1) Get water baptized (2) Ask Jesus to baptize (fill and immerse) you in the Holy Spirit (3) Pray Daily (4) Read the Bible everyday (5) Confess Jesus as Lord to others (6) Meet regularly with other Christians in church and Bible studies (7) Grow in Christ.

To be placed on our mailing list write us at:
CHRISTIAN COWBOYS & FRIENDS
P.O. Box 187, Blanco, Texas 78606 • (830) 386-4936

Miracles Among The Cowboys!

To be placed on our mailing list write us at:
Christian Cowboys & Friends
P.O. Box 187, Blanco, Texas 78606 • (830) 386-4936

Additional Teaching material by Ronnie Christian

- **Books**
  - Leadership, Followship, Relationship - $6.00 + $1.00 S&H
  - Hang On To Your Hope - $12.00 + $2.00 S&H
  - Miracles Among The Cowboys! - $12.00 + $2.00 S&H

We also publish
  - Christian Cowboys and Friends Teaching/Newsletter
    ten to twelve times per year

Suggested gift for this publication is $15.00 per year/$25.00 two years. Add $10.00 per year for Canada and $15.00 per year for other countries. Send "U.S." funds.

To get on mail list send request to Address below.

- **Cowboy Bible** - New American Standard Version with Rodeo artwork on the cover (you will get additional literature with your order) - $9.00
  <u>Notice:</u> Countries out of USA <u>must</u> send $16.00 "U.S. Funds" money order

Consider the above items for yourself or as a gift to a friend, co-workers or family members. Call, write, or e-mail.

Christian Cowboys and Friends
P.O. Box 187, Blanco, TX 78606
(830) 386-4936
Email: rcrodeo@christiancowboy.org
Website: www.christiancowboy.org

<u>Cowboy Partner</u> - Become a Cowboy Partner in this ministry by sending us out with finances and prayers to reach cowboys/cowgirls and others with the Good News of Jesus Christ. Our victory is in Jesus.

ORDER FORM
Great as a gift!
Order Books for family, friends, co-workers and others as a gift a witnessing tool for Jesus.

*Fill out the form below to order books
by Ronnie Christian*

# of books

_____ **Miracles Among The Cowboys!**
$12.00 + $2.00 S&H $_____

_____ **Hang On To Your Hope**
$12.00 + $2.00 S&H $_____

_____ **Leadership, Followship, Relationship**
$6.00 + $1.00 S&H $_____

TOTAL $_____

Order 10 or more and get 25% discount

**Send Check or Money Order to:
Christian Cowboys and Friends
P.O. Box 187
Blanco, TX 78606
(830) 386-4936**

Name_____

Address_____

State_____ Zip_____

CPSIA information can be obtained
at www.ICGtesting.com
Printed in the USA
FSOW02n0732040615
7652FS